Praise for the author

The author addresses an intriguing subject. Often I receive documents and presentations that do not really spur me into action. This book gives pragmatic advice, starting from concrete business situations. It is an enormous relief compared to the many handbooks that describe the theory and focus on information sharing. But in business, it's all about getting into results-oriented action. And that's what this book is all about.
Jan van den Nieuwenhuijzen, CEO, SD Worx

Poor communication destroys value. These losses are escalating as the pace of change accelerates and businesspeople struggle to set priorities in their packed 24/7 schedules. As Herman Vantrappen points out, the losses stem from the failure to convert intention into action. Implementation of the concepts in this valuable and overdue book could lead to a step change in the delivery of value. The author, with whom I have worked for 20 years, is himself a disciple of these critically important concepts: the few words or lines he writes in otherwise busy exchanges are frequently respected to be the most valuable.
Richard Clarke, former CEO, Arthur D. Little

Finally a book about how to write in such a way that business executives really read texts and act upon them. This book is of great value in these times of multi-media communication – and because there is always a shortage of time. It helps you increase the effectiveness of your memos, papers or even books because as a writer you are always trying to get your message across and ensure that its recipients will act accordingly.
Hans Smits, CEO, Port of Rotterdam Authority

This is not "just another book on good writing principles." It is an eminently readable book on effective communications. By focusing on the actionable purpose of our written communications, it should appeal to all of us, in business as well as other types of organizations. The author is frighteningly efficient in pointing at our usual writing sloppiness and recommending simple but powerful guidelines to make us think before writing and pay attention to all intended and unintended reactions to our texts. After reading it, you will look differently at the texts you receive... and much more critically at the ones you send. But you will have an invaluable and practical guide to produce quality texts and messages!
Professor Jean-Philippe Deschamps, IMD

The executive action writer: How to set your mind to crafting a text that evokes the response you want

ISBN: 1449572979
EAN-13: 9781449572976

The Executive Action Writer

How To Set Your Mind To Crafting A Text That Evokes The Response *You* Want

Herman J. Vantrappen

For JPD, MVR and KVT, coaches for life

Contents

Preface

Dear Reader,

You will forgive me for wondering whether undertaking to write a book about quality writing might reveal a masochistic undercurrent in my personality. Anything written less than perfectly in such a book risks unleashing the sarcasm that naturally resides in the mind of the professional book reviewer – and possibly in the minds of the book's readers.

Be that as it may, I undertook to write such book. While I have been a management consultant with a major strategy consulting firm for more than two decades, and an Editorial Board member and the editor-in-chief of its journal, *Prism*, for close to ten years, the trigger for this undertaking was not irritation with the lousy quality of many a text, whether written by a client or a colleague. The trigger was the combination of four other factors.

First, it was amazement about the apparent lack of shame among many text writers about the quality of their texts. I am not referring to literary quality here, but to the failure of the texts to incite the targeted readers to take the action that the writers intended them to take. I presume that many writers of business texts are simply unaware of what low quality means and entails. This book aims to raise awareness about the need for and benefit of high-quality writing.

The second factor that led to this book was puzzlement. Whether at high school, at university or on the job, many of us have had training courses about written communication skills. Nevertheless, the quality of texts remains very uneven. I presume that part of the explanation of this paradox lies in the emphasis that many courses put on the technical side of writing at the expense of the mental aspects. Good writing, I am convinced, is above all a state of mind. The second aim of this book is to provide writers with practical guidelines for setting their minds to making high-quality texts.

The third factor was a personal one: passion. While I always find writing to be hard work, I often also derive much pleasure from its results. The prospect of results fires the passion needed to keep going. With this book, I aim to share and transfer some of this passion to other people in business, who ordinarily equate writing only with drudgery.

The fourth factor, finally, was vanity. As Mark Twain said: "I was born modest; not all over, but in spots." So forgive me for admitting that one morning it dawned upon me that quite a few people of diverse plumage in my life have pointed to the considerable writing skills I appear to use, from the highly respectable CEO's pleasurable "Vintage Vantrappen" to my wife's titillating "You've such an incredible talent! Why don't you make more use of it?"

But back to real life. When I eventually decided to write this book, it had to be one that would be different from existing books on the subject. These share a number of characteristics. First of all, they usually focus on the technical construction of the text: the process steps to go through, the logical structure of the text, the style guidelines to follow, and the grammatical and linguistic requirements such as punctuation. Second, they invariably offer prescriptive models for different types of texts, such as a memo, a letter or a proposal, using perfect examples as support. Third, they tend to be long – sometimes excruciatingly long, running to up to 800 pages – and thus unwieldy. Their implied reader is a company employee sitting behind a desk and having oodles of time – as opposed to an intelligent businessperson always short of time (the segment that I expect you belong to, dear reader). Fourth, most of these books date from a time when web-based communications were not yet omnipresent and speed was less of the essence. Fifth, many of them are written by experts from academia or professional writers. No offense intended, but you have to have been a victim before you can be an instructor to the perpetrators. Finally, in an effort to be inoffensively didactic, they often end up devoid of irony, dry and boring, and you can't imagine a business executive settling down with them for a good read.

In other words, existing books explain in extensive detail how to write a technically flawless text using perfect examples as a model. Not this book. This book is conceived upon two premises. First, that most writers in business are fairly intelligent and always short of time. Second, that they generally do not need technical perfection for their texts to serve their purpose, i.e. to persuade the reader to take the action required. In those cases where a business text does need to be technically perfect (for example, when it is going into a commercial brochure), it will have to pass through a professional editor for finishing anyway, whether within the business or externally.

This book focuses on the writer's mindset rather than on the technical construction of the text. It offers practical guidelines rather than prescriptive models. It is deliberately short, using unfussy business language, and is written by a businessman with more than 20 years' experience of wrestling, both as a writer and a reader, with his own and others' purported words of wisdom.

In a nutshell, what I want to say is this: when you are about to write a text, allow yourself first to relax and think. Imagine yourself making a good cup of tea, leaning back and giving free rein to your creativity. That is what *The Executive Action Writer* is all about.

Publishers always declare that their business books are a "must-read for every CEO." This book is more modest and at the same time more ambitious. It is a "must-distribute by every CEO" to all managers throughout the organization because it will make business more effective and efficient.

But there is no greater stimulus than leaving the judgment about this book to you, dear reader. Your comments are warmly welcomed at herman@teawriter.com

Herman Vantrappen
Fall 2009

Meet The Executive Action Writer

Any discussion about a vocational skill – be it aquarelle painting, stand-up comedy or badminton playing – quickly turns to the question of nature versus nurture. Is the skillfulness an innate gift, or is it a technique that can be taught and learnt? While the debate on the subject isn't closed, the current consensus appears to embrace the idea that skillfulness is the result of the combination, matching and mutual reinforcement of gift and technique. It is like a farmer's harvest: the yield depends on the intrinsic fertility of the soil and the farmer's mastery of tilling techniques after years of experience.

The same question and answer in all likelihood apply to writing. Good writing certainly is a matter of technique, one that can be taught and trained, with the eventual result being influenced by the writer's innate gift. That said, good writing is more than the fruitful combination of gift and technique. Above all it is a state of mind. It is about being unforgiving with yourself about the quality of your writing. It is about taking pride in the precise formulation of a message so that you know it will strike a chord with your audience that resonates with your intent. Ultimately it is about experiencing an almost aesthetic satisfaction with the result and effect of your writing.

The above applies to all sorts of business texts, not just grand pieces of work such as an article in a journal, a corporate brochure or the annual CEO's message to all staff. It applies also to ordinary texts, whether an e-mail to a colleague, a letter to a prospective client or a one-page memo to your boss. Any text must be of high quality, with the effort being put into it obviously bearing a relationship to its context and purpose.

Some might argue that in today's fast-paced world of instant, omnipresent and byte-size hyper-communication, most texts are ephemeral by design, hence not worth the effort of thoughtful shaping. The vast majority of today's texts, so the argument goes, are meant and seen to be consumables and disposables. Certainly we are not advocating that each business text should be created as an awesome monument for future generations to admire. But we do believe that business will run much more efficiently if each writer in business invests a bit more effort in the quality of business texts.

Let's make the parallel with the concept of "total cost of ownership", abbreviated as TCO, which product manufacturers are familiar with. TCO considers not only the direct purchase cost of a product, such as a car, but also all other indirect costs over the entire life of the product, such as insurance, maintenance and repair, fuel consumption, taxes and disposal. Likewise, businesses should consider the "total cost of readership." A text may be quick, easy and cheap to produce for a writer, but what about the cost to business of readers who ignore, misunderstand or misinterpret the message? With today's omnipresent and instant communications infrastructure, the marginal cost of creating and communicating a text may be virtually nil, but what about the marginal benefit to its readers?

Against this backdrop, when you are about to write a text, the immediate question to ask yourself is whether you should write it in the first place. You can write a text at any time and place you fancy or happen to have a window of opportunity, but will your readers be better off with or without it? Once you have passed that test, you can set your mind to writing a high-quality text, i.e. creating a message that evokes the desired response from your readers.

The purpose of this book is to help you acquire the skills for writing high-quality business texts. We will explain a number of techniques. We also intend to stimulate a state of mind that will make you reject any text of your own that is not of high quality. Will you, through this book, become a Pulitzer Prize-winning writer? Maybe. That answer also depends on your innate talents. But the purpose of this book is not to grow award-winning writers. Its ultimate purpose is to make business more efficient.

To clarify this point, let's go back to the book's title, "The Executive Action Writer." Each of those words is chosen carefully:

- **"Writer", not "Writing."** The book is not about "writing" as an abstract subject. The book appeals to the individual businessperson, for whom writing is an everyday act (whether she likes it or not).

- **"Action Writer."** The book's basic premise is that, in business, any text message that a businessperson writes should eventually lead to action of some sort by the people to whom it is addressed. Writing that does not lead to action is waste.

- **"Executive."** The adjective relates to both "writer" and "action". The book is about executives requiring others – through a written message – to take action. The term "executive" is used in a broad sense, meaning not only senior managers but managers and professional staff at all levels.

By the same token, the book's sub-title, "How To Set Your Mind To Crafting A Text That Evokes The Response *You* Want," contains four promises:

- **"How To."** The book is neither an abstract academic treatise nor a dreary technical manual. It uses real-life examples to which you as a businessperson can relate, and it gives practical advice you can apply immediately. There is no magic to writing – it is a matter of mindset and craftsmanship.
- **"Set Your Mind."** The first of the book's two basic messages is that writing a business text that leads to action is a matter not so much of technical perfection (construction, grammar, punctuation, etc.) but mindset – you have to make a mental switch so that you will really feel bad about a text of yours if it is not of high quality.
- **"Crafting."** The book's other basic message is that high-quality writing is also about craftsmanship. There is no escape: if you want your text to lead to action, you must be willing to carve, chisel and polish it until it stands as it should.
- **"*You* want."** If you write high-quality texts, you will be a more successful businessperson. You will be able to make other people act in the way you want them to. A high-quality text is one that evokes the response *you* want.

In this book we use the term "business" as a generic name to refer to enterprises, non-profit entities, government bodies and other organizations that have stakeholders, members and a structure for achieving a shared purpose. The book should serve white-collar people in businesses and other organisations who write regularly in their professional lives because they have some managerial responsibility or are in an advisory support function.

The term "business text" in this book means any message that requires direct or indirect action from the reader. An example of a direct action is the reader's approval of the proposal contained in the text. An example of an indirect action is a change of the reader's opinion induced by the text and which, at some point in the future, will inform his decisions and actions. A business text can be of various types, such as a report, a presentation, a web page, a memo, an e-mail, a speech or an article. It is usually received by its readers as something to be read on a sheet of paper or screen, but it could also be something to be listened to. We use the terms "readers" or "audience" to refer to the variety of recipients of a text. These can be a single individual, a group or a multitude or sequence of these.

The book is divided into two parts. Part A channels the writer's mind before starting. Each of the first six chapters corresponds to one reflex a writer should have when preparing a business text. Each reflex is summarized as a question for self-assessment (see Table 1). The seventh chapter provides a summary of these reflexes.

Part B provides practical help. It presents five examples of authentic poor-quality texts, assesses each of them by answering the six questions raised in Part A, and suggests re-worked versions. It leads you through practical analytical steps that encourage quality-based thinking and writing, and helps you to acquire the skills to practise both. After reading and applying the guidelines in this book, you should be much more confident about your texts and be able to say: "Gone are the days of sending a business text to people and not getting them to act the way *I* wanted them to act."

Table 1: Six questions for self-assessment

Chapter 1. Get To Know Your Subject Intimately *Explains how to answer: "Do I know enough about the subject I am writing about to produce a logical text that will convince my readers?"*
Chapter 2. Segment Your Audience *Explains how to answer: "Have I segmented my audience (who will or may read my text, now and in the future), and have I thought through which messages may be harmful if read by any of these segments?"*
Chapter 3. Focus On Your Purpose For Writing – And Your Audience's For Reading *Explains how to answer: "Have I made sure – through the packaging, length, lead-in, form and conclusion of my text – that it will stand out from the noise, and that my readers will pigeonhole it in the 'read and act now' category?"*
Chapter 4. Take Into Account The Mode Of Consumption *Explains how to answer: "Have I made sure that my text will reach my readers for consumption at an auspicious time and place?"*
Chapter 5. Use Form To Your Advantage *Explains how to answer: "Have I given my text the structure, visual appearance and technical finish required to make a good first impression, enable the various segments in the audience to assimilate its content in a reader-friendly way, and neutralize the nit-pickers?"*
Chapter 6. Work And Work Again On Your Text *Explains how to answer: "Have I used clear logic and precise wording so that my readers get the same meaning from my text as I put in?"*

If you are still not wholly convinced of the merit of reading this book, have a look at the sales pitch below.

If you had not started reading this book today, I imagine you would have gone to your office, switched on your computer and opened your e-mail box. Let's do a simple test. Ignoring spam, assume there are ten genuine messages: from a colleague, a customer, your boss – you name it. Each of these sent you a message, not for fun of course, but because they wanted you to do something: give your opinion, share some data or take some other action. And here is the test: for how many of these ten will you act exactly as the author presumably wanted you to act? I am pretty sure it will be less than half. You will misinterpret some messages; some you will decide to read later; and still others you will plainly ignore. What a waste of effort and time from their authors!

But let's turn the tables. What happens to texts *you* write, whether an e-mail, a memo to a colleague, a letter to a customer, a presentation to a board or any other business message? Even if you score better, say seven out of ten, that still leaves three of your messages that fail to achieve their purpose of evoking the response *you* wanted. What a terrible waste.

The good news is that there are simple ways to improve your score to 100 per cent. There are six reflexes that you as a businessperson can cultivate and that will help you create high-quality texts – that is, texts that make other people act in the way *you* want them to. Rest assured, by these six reflexes I don't mean technical stuff like: "Should I use the active rather than the passive tense?" or "Can I use a semicolon here?" Writing a business text that leads to action is not a matter of technical perfection but of mindset – you have to make a mental switch so that you will feel really bad about a text of yours that is not of high quality. This book will give you the six keys that will enable you to make that switch – starting tomorrow.

Part A

SET YOUR MIND

The first of this book's two basic messages is that writing a business text that leads to action is a matter not so much of technical perfection but of mindset – you have to make a mental switch so that you will really feel bad about a text of yours if it is not of high quality. In this first part of the book, we present six reflexes that you can cultivate and that will help you make high-quality texts, i.e. messages that evoke the desired response from your audience.

1

Get To Know Your Subject Intimately

The central tenet of this book is that a high-quality text is one that evokes a response from the reader that corresponds with the intent of the author. Writing a business text is about persuading others to take action: to share some information with you, to make a decision, to change opinion, to work differently, to acknowledge completion of an action you had to undertake, etc.

Your challenge then is to make your thoughts, words and sentences materialize into a convincing story. It will be very hard to do so unless the logic that underpins your message is clear in your mind first (see Exhibit 1). Before you pick up your pen or hit your keyboard, you should visualize in your mind from which combination of arguments your intended conclusion will flow. That does not necessarily mean that the physical sequence of the statements in your eventual text should strictly follow the original logic in your mind. Depending on your readers and purpose, you may shuffle the arguments, repeat some, leave out others, etc. But at least in your mind, the logic should be crystal clear.

Exhibit 1: Requirements to make a convincing story

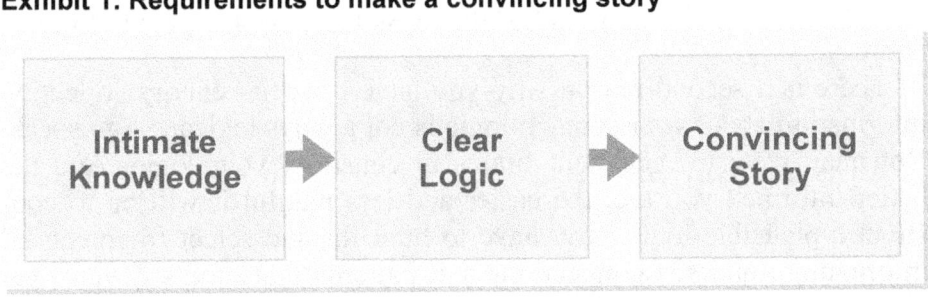

KNOW MORE ABOUT THE SUBJECT THAN YOUR READERS DO

"Be logical" is more easily said than done. What helps to be convincingly logical in your argumentation is to (get to) know the subject of your text intimately well. Before you start structuring your arguments, familiarize yourself well with the subject you are writing about.

Imagine that you passionately believe in the potential for your company to enter, say, the Pakistani fertilizer industry, and that you have been pleading with your management to do so. They finally succumb to your plea and throw the ball back: "If you are so convinced, why don't you make us an investment proposal?" You would probably go to great lengths to get all the facts together, build a rock-solid story, and anticipate any counter-arguments your management might raise. You wouldn't give them any chance of surprising you with any facts unknown to you. You would want to be the expert on the subject matter.

You should show the same basic ardor in getting to know your subject intimately whenever you write a text, even if it is a much less weighty one than that in the above example. There are two reasons for doing so. First, at least some of your readers are likely to have opinions that deviate from, or even oppose, yours. The only way to convince them is to have arguments that are new or are used in novel combinations. Even more mundanely, if you use only arguments that everybody knows already, why would anybody change their opinion and act? And if you overlook important arguments, you invite a better-informed reader to expose the holes in your reasoning and thus discredit your entire story.

There is a second reason why you have to spend energy collecting information about your subject: logic is not always logical, so to speak. You may have to rack your brains to construct your logic. And the better informed you are, the easier and less painful it will be to construct a plausible logic. You have to hunt for and select fragments of information, and see connections and patterns that others haven't yet seen, but which you will show them through your text. As they read your text, you want them to discover – without much effort and to their own great delight – the message exactly as you wanted it.

You should compare yourself to the creator of a jigsaw puzzle – one that is easy to put together yet with an outcome that pleasantly surprises the person doing it. You first create the puzzle image. Then you jigsaw the image into meaningful pieces and put them into a box. The person opening the box will be proud of the speed with which he manages to put the pieces together, and pleasantly surprised by the image he discovers.

FIGHT THE TEMPTATION OF INTELLECTUAL LAZINESS

You have to familiarize yourself with the subject of your text – the more intimately the better. And there is a mental hurdle. With a grain of exaggeration, we could say that many business people are intellectually lazy, at least when it comes to writing. They don't take the time to ask themselves: What do I know about the subject? What do I know that others don't? What should I know but don't? What do others know that I don't? Once you have the answers to these questions, it is much easier to see and plug the holes in your subject knowledge.

A good example to clarify this point is the speech you are asked to write and make at a farewell drink for a colleague. You probably would not accept to do it if you didn't know the colleague well – possibly even better than any other colleague does. And still you would go hunting for additional pieces of information to weave into your speech, with which you could surprise and impress the fêted colleague, your other colleagues and, let's be honest, possibly even your boss. You would then piece the various fragments together into a logical storyline – logical not so much in the Cartesian sense but in a way that will capture and keep the attention of your audience from start to finish. And what keeps you writing is the anticipation of the laughter and handclapping accompanying your oration.

For a speech, it sounds obvious what to do to do it well. Similar fervor should go into writing any business text.

USE EMOTION TO LUBRICATE YOUR LOGIC

Writing is acting. You have to dissolve into a persona that is both you and not you. As when acting, you have to put emotion into writing. In a business text, emotion is the lubricant of logic. Emotion gives that flash of inspiration that makes a text flow well. But the emotion is played and controlled. If you write a text on the basis of uncontrolled emotion, you're likely to regret it soon. We have all read if not written that fuming e-mail that we know the author is going to regret no later than having pushed the Send button. There is indeed a fundamental difference between putting emotion into something and being emotional. Putting emotion into something is playing Faust on stage; being emotional is leading yourself to doom for real.

Putting emotion into the act of writing doesn't mean the resulting text itself should have a theatrical style. The style of a text depends on the audience, the intent and the mode of consumption of the text, as we will explain in a later chapter.

LEARN FROM SOCIAL PSYCHOLOGY AND BEHAVIORAL ECONOMICS

There are two masterly business books to which we will refer regularly in this and the following chapters: Robert Cialdini's *Influence: The Psychology of Persuasion* and Richard Thaler's *Nudge: Improving Decisions about Health, Wealth, and Happiness* (co-authored with Cass Sunstein). Neither of these books deals with business writing per se, and the two authors have totally different backgrounds and research interests. Nevertheless both contain insights that are highly relevant and applicable to the subject of business writing – and of course to many other subjects, which makes both books highly recommendable (see full details in the bibliography at the end of this book).

Cialdini is a social psychologist who is doing research on the psychology of compliance, i.e. the factors that cause one person to say yes to another person. He explains, for example, how a super car salesman succeeds in selling so many more cars than an ordinary salesman, or how one waiter succeeds in extracting tips from restaurant patrons that are a multiple of those his colleague waiter in the very same restaurant gets.

Thaler is a behavioral economist who is doing research on choice architectures, i.e. the system that helps people to improve their ability to select options that will make them better off. He explains, for example, how public policy makers can nudge – not mandate – people into saving more for their retirement, or how government can increase organ donations from deceased people.

However, the two books have a common starting point: that in many situations individuals – unwillingly or even unknowingly – make pretty bad decisions because the bad decision is easier to make than the good one. Cialdini explains how people often comply automatically and mindlessly with requests made of them, and appear willing to say yes without thinking first. Thaler explains that, contrary to common belief, people do not always make choices that are in their best interest.

We make pretty bad decisions from time to time because, busy as we are, we cannot afford to think too long about every decision we have to make in the complex world that is ours. We cannot afford each time to identify, assess and weigh all the factors that, in theory, should inform our decision. As a consequence, we make fairly automatic decisions, based on past experience or just one clue that is presented to us. Cialdini observes that often we take the first piece of good-enough evidence that comes along to make a decision, especially when we don't have the time, energy or cognitive abilities to think everything through. Thaler explains that, when confronted with a choice, we rely on rules of thumb that in many cases have proven to be sensible yet which, for the choice at hand, lead us astray.

If the above is true, it follows that some people, often but not always well-intentioned, will take advantage of our automatic responses to make us behave in a way that benefits *them* (too). It has been scientifically proven that these people, in order to trigger our automatic response, use a combination of subtle yet simple tactics. One of them is what social scientists call "framing". Choices depend, in part, on the way in which problems are stated. Cialdini shows that two people asking essentially the same favor from a third person may still evoke a different reaction. One may get a rejection and the other an acceptance, simply because they asked the favor in a slightly different fashion. Thaler notes that small and apparently insignificant differences in how others present things to us can change our behavior enormously.

Imagine your boss has asked you to set up a small team to determine the specifications of a new system. You are sending a mail to a number of colleagues you know well, to enquire about their interest in being part of the team. You could ask them in two different ways: "Would you like to be part of the team?" or "What contribution could you make to the team?" You are likely to get different answers, because you "framed" the questions differently.

This leads us to the relevance of Cialdini's and Thaler's concepts for this book. Remember its purpose: to show how to evoke a response from the readers of your texts that corresponds with your intent. You want to make your readers comply with your requests for action. You want to nudge them into acting as you wish. Clearly you do not want to mislead, deceive or manipulate your readers; you simply want to convince, persuade and facilitate.

Let's look at a number of compliance tactics you can use when writing a text. The more you familiarize yourself intimately with the subject of your text, the more successful these tactics will be.

MAKE YOURSELF LIKABLE TO YOUR READERS

Assume that you and your colleague have the same capabilities and roles, and are sending the very same text to your common boss. Imagine the unlikely situation that your boss one way or another likes your colleague more than he likes you. There is a fair chance that he will respond more rapidly or more positively to your colleague than he does to you. No surprise there.

Now assume that the two of you are sending a text not to your boss, but to an outsider who doesn't know either of you at all. As a consequence, he has no ground a priori to distinguish between you and your colleague in terms of like or dislike. Suppose now that the message in your and your colleague's text is the same, but there are subtle differences in its form or wording, so that your colleague seems to be more likable than you. Again your colleague is likely to obtain the more rapid or positive response.

If you make yourself likable to the person you are addressing through your text, he is more likely to give the response you wanted to evoke. This sounds like obvious advice, yet it is regularly ignored. Often unknowingly, we lead the readers of our texts not to like us as much as we would wish, for reasons that have nothing to do with the substance of our message: a misspelled name, an off-putting term, an irreverent statement, an awkward illustration, etc. The question, then, is how you can make yourself more likable.

APPEAR SIMILAR TO YOUR READERS

One important way to make yourself likable to your readers is to make yourself look similar to them. If we have the choice between a similar or a dissimilar person, Cialdini notes, we tend to follow the lead of the former. It is no surprise then that people who want us to follow their lead will make themselves appear similar to us, for example by claiming or referring to similar backgrounds or interests. Cialdini also warns that it is easy to fabricate a thin layer of similarity.

Imagine you are writing a letter to a class of graduating students, inviting them to the recruitment event your company is organizing. Obviously your intent is to generate maximum attendance by the students, or by a subset with a specific profile. In your letter you would certainly do the normal thing: explain why your company is so great, why the students are so unique and why the event is so special. But one other thing you could do to maximize attendance is to make yourself *as an individual* look similar to them and consequently more likable.

In order to find authentic and meaningful similarities, you will have to familiarize yourself with your subject, e.g. the students, their courses or their teachers. It shouldn't take much time – mostly just a bit of thinking and imagination. For example, if you happen to be an alumnus of that school, you could look up who today's teachers are, identify those who were already teaching there when you were a student, and construct a very short, amusing anecdote around a notable one; you could start your letter with: "When I was sitting in Professor Zweistein's class back in 1995 …"

The readers of your letter may find you are similar to them, consequently like you, and consequently respond positively to your letter. The fact that you are seen to have taken the effort to personalize your letter can't but increase their liking. Note also that you did not *fake* similarity. With a bit of research, you will always find some *genuine* similarity.

CONFER PRAISE ON YOUR READERS

Another way to make yourself likable to your readers is to flatter them. You may think this is a ploy too easy and transparent to be credible, but it works. Cialdini demonstrates that we believe a compliment almost instinctively and we like the individual who makes it, even when we sense it is not sincere.

Let's go back to the example of you being asked to set up a small team and sending a mail to a number of colleagues to enquire about their interest in joining the team. If you add a small compliment (e.g. "When we worked together last time, I very much appreciated the candor with which you shared your reservations about …"), they will like you better, and they will be more inclined to say yes.

When applying this tactic, you have to do a bit of research first. You may want to find out what appeals to your reader's sense of pride. And you have to find a genuine link between the reader and the subject of your text in order to make your compliment credible. Don't overdo it – you can appeal to your reader's vanity but don't stretch his gullibility to breaking point.

BRING BAD NEWS WHEN RELEVANT AND ACCOMPANIED BY A SOLUTION

One way to avoid making yourself dislikable is not to bring bad news. Cialdini notes that reason tells us to distinguish between the *messenger* of bad news and the *cause* of bad news, but nevertheless we dislike the person who brings us unpleasant information because we still associate him with it. That raises a dilemma because the willingness and ability of a company's managers both to bring and handle bad news are said to be one of the signs of a healthy company culture. Furthermore sincerity and courage one way or the other always figure prominently on the list of characteristics of great business leaders. So what should you do?

First, bring bad news only if it is relevant to the reader, i.e. if she needs it to be able to take the action you want her to take. While this may sound pretty basic, you probably also know some people around you who seem to relish being in the news by bringing bad news. They seem to love having a scoop at any price. They seem to believe that the advertising company's saying "any publicity is good publicity" also applies to them as an individual. While Stanford researcher Alan Sorensen has proven that the saying is true in the case of book reviews (that is, even negative reviews lead to increases in sales), you should resist the temptation to put it in practice through your own texts.

Even more importantly, if you do have to bring bad news, bring solutions too. If you send a text to a reader, you do so because you want her to take some action. Especially if the text contains bad news, include suggestions for alternative actions or be helpful in any other way. As he talks about choice architecture, Thaler recommends helping people map and select options by making the information about the options more comprehensible. For you to be able to provide comprehensible and relevant information to your readers, once again you will have to get to know the subject of your text intimately well.

2

Segment Your Audience

A business text is a message that is written in order to lead to action by its readers, collectively called its audience. But an audience is rarely homogenous. It often consists of various individuals or groups of individuals whom you expect to act each in their own way. Furthermore, your text may be read by people whom you never intended to reach. The familiar example is the mail you send to someone, who replies to you, and thereby copies it without further thought to the person who, in your mind, should be the last to read your original mail.

In other words, there is a primary, secondary and tertiary audience. The primary audience is the segment that you address formally and directly. The secondary audience is the segment that you address indirectly, be it intentionally or unintentionally. The tertiary audience is the segment that you do not want to address at all but that may still happen to read your text. As a consequence, for your text to evoke a response from your readers that resonates with your intent, you should segment your audience, and write the text keeping in mind the various segments that will or may read it.

RECOGNIZE DIVERSE INTERESTS WITHIN YOUR FORMAL AUDIENCE

The first segment includes the people who are your formal audience, such as the addressee of a memo or the participants in a presentation. Obviously, that segment may consist of sub-segments with diverse interests.

Suppose, for example, that you make a presentation of the findings of an assessment of an acquisition target to a potential investor. Your primary audience may include not only the investment manager of the investor company, but also the commercial banker who is considering lending money to the investor to finance the acquisition. Clearly, the investment manager and commercial banker have different interests, but you still want them to act according to your intent. You will succeed in that only if you have taken their different interests into account when writing your presentation.

REMEMBER THAT INDIRECT READERS MAY BE MORE IMPORTANT

The second segment includes the people who are not your formal audience but whom you still expect and maybe even want to read your text. They may be more important in terms of ultimate decision-making than your primary audience. As the purpose of your text is to evoke action, you will have to persuade your secondary audience as much as or even more than your primary audience.

For example, you may expect the addressee of a memo to forward it to a third party, whether you like it or not. Or take the above-mentioned example of a presentation about an acquisition target. The investment manager to whom you have presented your findings in a two-hour session may forward your document to a senior Investment Committee, whose members have not been involved in the process before, have no clue about the acquisition target, and can devote only ten minutes to the subject. You had better make sure that your document – both through its content and form – can be appreciated by the Investment Committee members too. The obvious thing to do is to add an Executive Summary that includes facts about the acquisition target that may be superfluous for your primary audience – the investment manager and commercial banker – but instrumental for making your secondary audience – the Investment Committee – follow you. Form-wise, you should make life easy for the investment manager, for example by separating the document into two parts, one part being aimed at the Investment Committee.

ANTICIPATE THE READING OF YOUR TEXT BY MYSTERY PEOPLE

The third segment is the mystery audience. It includes the people you do not intend to reach either directly or indirectly, whom you sometimes wouldn't want to read your text at all, whom you may not know, and whom you may not know received your text. But, with today's communications technology, any text can be scanned, forwarded and put onto the worldwide web in a matter of seconds, for anybody and everybody to look at. In cyberspace, Murphy's infamous law reads as follows: "Anybody who must not read your text will read it." By the way, you don't have to be a cynic to put little confidence in the stamp "confidential" that you may have put above your text. It is safe to assume the worst when writing your text.

As a consequence, the challenge is to make a text that is explicit and clear to your primary audience yet will not create collateral damage among the mystery audience. Take again the above-mentioned example of the presentation about the acquisition target. Your assessment of the acquisition target may include, unobtrusively, a critical assessment of the target's top manager. Assume that the investor does acquire the company, and then, without intending mischief, passes your presentation on to the acquired company's top manager. Your assessment of her may have been frank and fair, but that doesn't mean you want her to read your assessment, certainly not if you intend to do business with her in the future.

DISTINGUISH BETWEEN HARMFUL AND HARMLESS MESSAGES

Thus, when writing a text, it pays to think through the various segments within your audience, and which messages from your text could be harmful if they reach them. You can then decide which messages to keep, reformulate or remove. Whether you do this exercise explicitly and in-depth, or implicitly and superficially of course depends on the situation (see Exhibit 2).

Clearly you should keep the messages that are harmless to all segments. Vice versa, you should reformulate or remove messages that are harmful to all segments. You should also reformulate a message that is harmful to your primary and/or secondary audience yet presumably harmless to your (unknown) tertiary audience.

The difficulty comes with messages that are harmless to your primary and/or secondary audience yet possibly harmful to your often unknown tertiary audience. If you reformulate or remove the message, you risk not getting the true meaning of your message across to your core audience. This would have been the case in the above example with the critical assessment of the target's top manager. The only way out is to use your common sense. For example, for topics that you should reasonably know are sensitive, you could put an indirect reference in your text, and give details to your primary audience verbally. In the above example about the target's top manager, you could write: "A more in-depth assessment of the company's senior management is called for in order to remove any concerns about their ability to realize the set objectives."

Exhibit 2: Sorting messages by segment and potential harm

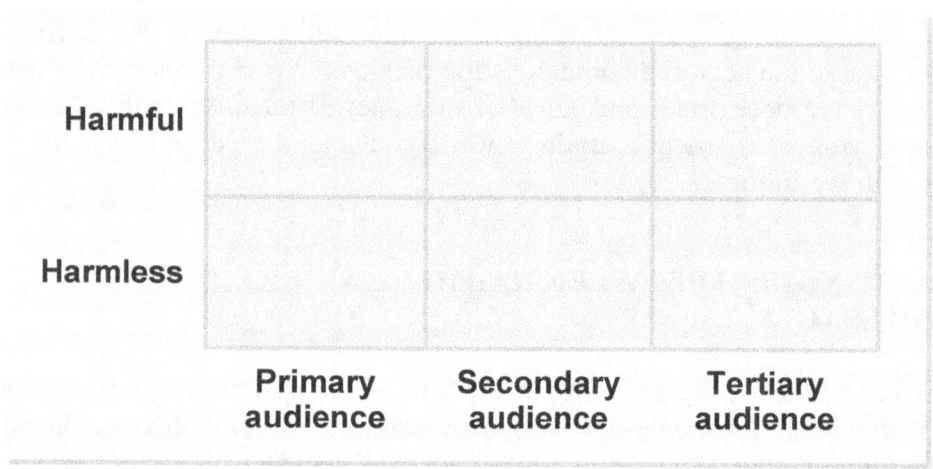

COURT THE SENTINELS STANDING BETWEEN YOU AND YOUR READERS

It is one thing to take into account the segments in your audience when writing a text. It is quite another to *get* your text to your audience, as it may be guarded by sentinels – people standing between you and your audience and filtering incoming texts. The classic example is the assistant who reads and channels a manager's mail. You may have to modify the content and/or form of your text simply to pass through these sentinels. Know who these sentinels are, and make it easy for them to understand the purpose of your text, so that they decide not to filter it out. In some cases it may be even more effective to address your text to the sentinel directly, asking her to forward your text to her boss. You may even want to call her first to announce and explain the impending arrival of a text.

If your text has to reach your audience through e-mail, be aware of the existence of virtual sentinels in the form of spam filters. Even if your e-mail gets through your audience's spam filter, it may have been marked as "suspect." And don't blame your audience for robotically deleting all "suspect" mails from senders whose names don't ring a bell. That may be another reason to call the person or her assistant first.

KEEP IN MIND THE SHELF LIFE OF YOUR TEXT

Time is an additional consideration to the segmentation of your audience. While many texts are written, consumed and disposed of within a short time period, others are put on a shelf for future re-use, without you knowing. On still other occasions, you purposefully intend your text to have a long shelf life, for example when you are writing a policy document. For each of those instances, you should consider how to write your text such that it will be correctly understood and/or stay relevant over its entire potential lifecycle.

Let's continue the above-mentioned example of the presentation about the acquisition target. When the acquisition transaction is closed, your presentation probably ends up along with many others somewhere in a box. But imagine that three years later, the same company is sold again, to another investor. It is not impossible that your presentation of yore will be made available to that new investor. Certainly if your name is attached to it, you want to be sure that the new audience interprets your original document correctly. For that purpose, it may be important, for example, to have in your original document a page clearly describing the context, purpose, timing and scope of your assessment of the acquisition target.

3

Focus On Your Purpose For Writing – And Your Audience's For Reading

In business writing, we are always leading our readers to take reasoned action. We want the readers to respond as we intended. So when you start writing, you should already have clear answers in your mind to two questions. First, what do you want to achieve with your text? Second, why would anyone want to read it? While the answer to the former question may turn out to be straightforward, the latter may prove more challenging. Even if you have a perfectly valid reason for writing, your efforts may be futile if you cannot persuade your audience to read your text (see Exhibit 3).

Exhibit 3: Matching purpose and reason

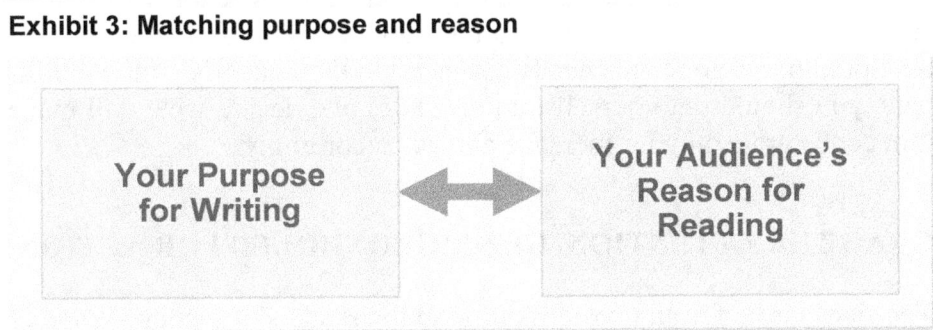

DO THE WORK FOR YOUR READERS – WHY SHOULD THEY READ IT?

Let's take the example of an e-mail that you have received and would like to forward to another interested party within your organization. You could simply forward the e-mail with the typical heading "for your information." But you provide no context or meaning in a flat "fyi." Information is useful only if it leads to action. So you should spell out in your e-mail, albeit extremely briefly, the use of the forwarded information to the recipient, and the action you expect or suggest taking after reading it.

Here is an example of an improved "fyi" message: "The other day you mentioned to me that you are working on the launch of SuperWidget. I came across the attached document that describes a similar product launched by MegaRival. Table 3, which compares the MegaRival product features with those of competitor products, could be particularly useful for optimizing the definition of SuperWidget." This is not being pedantic – it never hurts to remind the reader of your reasons for forwarding the information and creating a context for doing so.

Why, then, do so many of us forward e-mails with the dreaded "fyi"? We want to appear cooperative, without overdue effort on our part. Unless the information is indeed useful and seen as such by the recipient, these self-serving initiatives are annoying. In today's environment of "infoflation", restraint and reader-friendliness are scarce and commendable commodities.

Liken the relationship between a writer and his readers to that of supplier and customer. Your customer deserves your full attention and a tailored message for his needs. Even when the reader is your subordinate, you should put yourself into his shoes and decide what will make him concentrate on your message and act accordingly.

GRAB THE ATTENTION, GET PIGEONHOLED FOR ACTION

The first hurdle for any writer is to grab the readers' attention. Whether you like it or not, the readers of your text will mentally pigeonhole it into one of several possibly damning categories as soon as they receive it: "Ignore and ditch", "read later", "read now but harmless – no action", "read and act now", or other variants of the above. You may feel harshly judged, but you have only yourself to blame if your text does not fall into the last category. Text value is in the eye of the reader.

GET READ BECAUSE OF YOUR PERSONAL BRAND

The reader's sorting process starts with who wrote the piece. In every organization there are blighted individuals whose messages are systematically deleted by all and sundry without being read. By the same token, we all know of others whose words we ignore at our peril because when they write they mean business (irrespective of organizational hierarchy).

A writer is like any supplier peddling his wares to customers and trying to make his brand stand out in the crowd. All of us have a personal brand which we can rely on to get noticed and to build loyalty among our readers. If the brand image gets damaged and people lose confidence in you as an actionable item, recovery is hard. Be economical with e-mails and other texts, and stay with the good communicator crowd. Don't be a graffiti artist with your signature all over town but no one but yourself to admire it.

GET READ BECAUSE YOU PACKAGED THE MESSAGE RIGHT

As well as writer reputation, the way you package the message has a strong bearing on what the reader does with it because this sets the reader's first and often definitive impression. The content may remain invariable, but the title, the style of the first sentence or paragraphs as well as text form and mode of consumption should draw your readers' attention to you.

Consider the newspaper article analogy: its title, sub-title, lead-in and occasional picture will strongly influence whether it is noticed and fully read. In the same way, think about a job interview: The first ten seconds are often decisive and if the candidate messes up, it is very hard to recapture the lost ground with the interviewer. Once we have formed an initial impression, we bend all the other signals we receive about the candidate to fit that mould. Think carefully how to package your message since off-putting packaging could put you at a disadvantage before your reader even starts.

K.I.S.S. AND YOUR READERS STAY ENGAGED

Once you have caught your readers' attention, your challenge is how to keep it. So make life easy for them – keep it simple and stupid (KISS).

KEEP YOUR TEXT SHORT

Most business texts are too long for the purpose they serve, discouraging the reader from reading on and failing to get the essence of the message across. Therefore, if a certain piece of information is important but not critical, remove it from the body of your text into an appendix, a separate text window or another document. Similarly, don't bury critical information where your reader cannot find it easily. Put essential information in the body of an e-mail, not in an attachment that the recipient has to open first. For example, when mailing an invitation for a lecture you are giving, put the outline of your lecture and the explanation of how to get to the venue into an attachment, but make sure that the date appears in the body of your mail too.

GET TO YOUR WANTED RESPONSE QUICKLY

Get quickly to the point and do it in the very first sentence of your text if you can. In most instances, you should state the conclusion or action required at the start of your text so that the reader knows why you are addressing him – and why he should read on.

Suppose, for example, that you are the sales manager of a hand disinfectants producer, and plan to send a letter to a prospective customer with a request to see you. Make it clear very early in your letter that the purpose of your letter is to get her agreement to see you. Do not start off with some description of the context ("... the incidence of infectious diseases has been growing ..."), the problem ("... it has been shown that person-to-person contamination occurs primarily in offices ...") or your credentials ("... we are the leading producer, having won the industry award for excellence ..."). Chances are high that you are telling the reader things she already knows or that you are giving her the impression that you're stealthily trying to sell her something she doesn't want. Either way, your letter is irritating and she risks ditching it before finishing the first paragraph. It is better to start off with your request and afterwards add (as needed and possibly in an attachment) information about context, problem or credentials.

KEEP A TIGHT REIN

Use shape and form to keep your audience on a tight rein as they glide effortlessly through your text. You want the reader to read all parts of your text – otherwise you should not have put them in. We will come back to the shape and form of a high-quality text in Chapter 5.

PERSUADE YOUR READERS TO COMPLY WITH YOUR REQUEST

Once you have caught the readers' attention and as you take them through your text, you still have to provoke action, i.e. persuade them to act as you intended. For that purpose you can use a combination of tactics.

EXPLOIT THE POWER OF PERCEPTUAL CONTRAST

The negotiation tactic of asking for more than you need and eventually settling for what you really need is as old as the street. Cialdini describes the truly gifted negotiator as one who knows perfectly what his starting position should be: high enough so that he can afford to make a series of reciprocal concessions and still end up with the result he had targeted from the beginning; but not too high to make the other party immediately discard his offer as ludicrous. Thaler confirms the evidence that as long as you are reasonable you often get more if you ask for more.

You can also apply this tactic to your texts. For example, suppose your boss asks you to make an appraisal of the future outlook of a product line. In your report you would like to include historic sales figures for the last three years. For that purpose you are sending a request to the – always overworked – financial controller. In your mail to her, you could just ask her what you really need. Or you could ask her, in addition, to provide the breakdown of sales by region, knowing well that the extra information is not essential for you and that it would be very difficult for her to provide it. When she responds that she cannot provide the breakdown, you can "settle" for the figures for the totals.

A variant of that tactic is to insinuate that what you are asking is small beer compared to what you could have asked, what you asked in the past, or what you are asking from someone else. For example, in the above request to the controller, you could write: "Rest assured, I am not asking you to provide the breakdown by region, but only the totals for the last three years" or "I realize it may be quite difficult to get the breakdown by region, but if at least you could provide me the totals for the last three years" or "I admit that last month I requested you to do quite a bit of work for me already – thanks again for that, it was very helpful – but now I am only asking for the sales figures of the last three years."

All these tactics make use of the phenomenon that psychologists call "perceptual contrast." When we make judgments, we don't make absolute judgments but judge in comparison with something else. The tactics also exploit the common human tendency called "anchoring": to be biased by one piece of information when making decisions. In this context, Thaler explains that anchors serve as nudges.

Of course, you should use these tactics judiciously. There is a thin line between attempting to be smart and being seen as devious. In a business environment, most readers of your texts are people with whom you have a continuing relationship. If you make people feel taken in, your reputation and personal brand will suffer. Next time they may discount your texts. In other words, if you ask for more than you need, you may get more than you want.

SCRATCH YOUR READERS' BACKS

In businesses as in other social settings, give-and-take behavior is important grease for the normal functioning of the system. We respond to another individual's request partly because we hope and expect that he will respond to ours in the future. In your texts you can appeal to this sense of mutual favors in various ways.

The most direct way is to include something in your text that your reader may find immediately valuable. For example, in the above request to the controller, you could add: "By the way, as I was collecting material for my report, I came across a website (www....) showing an interesting benchmark analysis of the financial performance of company A, B and C, which you may find quite useful." Less directly you could subtly remind your reader of things you have done for her in the past, or provide the hint that she can always call on you in the future.

Cialdini refers to this give-and-take as reciprocity. He points to the immense power of gifts or favors to produce feelings of obligation. If you provide a favor prior to the request to your reader, you will stimulate him to respond to it. Most interestingly, Cialdini notes that this feeling of indebtedness exists even if the favor is uninvited, unwanted, and small compared to the favor you are requesting from the recipient. The reason that sometimes we provide a larger favor than we received is to be free of any feeling of debt.

APPEAL TO YOUR READERS' INCLINATION TO LOOK CONSISTENT

Imagine that you have been tasked with the publishing of your company's monthly internal newsletter. You need to ask for contributions from people in all of your company's departments. You know that if you broadcast a mail with your request, the response rate will be fairly low. Instead you could identify individuals in each department whom you suspect would be good sources of information and reasonably compliant, and send a personalized request to each of them. For the first edition of the newsletter, you should ask a small favor only, so as to increase the response rate: "I am not asking for much. A three-line description of the single most important event that took place in your department in the past month would be great." The next month, you ask for a bit more: "Last month you provided an excellent description of the family-day event in your department. It would be great if you could write a similar description of the events that took place this month." And the month after, you start calling your source "our regular contributor" and you include him in the newsletter column with the names of the "department correspondents."

The example shows how you can evoke a response from an individual by asking first for a small commitment and then building on it to obtain increasingly bigger commitments. According to Cialdini, the force that drives this escalation is our obsession with being and with being seen to be consistent. As a consequence, we explain to ourselves the reasons why we made the initial commitment and why we should commit ourselves further. The more our initial commitment has been visible to others, the stronger the force to look like a consistent person will be.

This tactic is even more effective when you use the small, initial commitment to make a person change his self-image, as was attempted in the above example through the use of "our regular contributor" and, for everybody to read in the newsletter, "our department correspondent." Once you have changed a person's self-image in line with your purpose, it will be much easier to persuade him to comply with your further requests. He will comply because he wants to look consistent with the self-image. As Cialdini notes, this tactic works especially well if the commitments are active, public and effortful.

Another way to apply this tactic is to refer to past requests and responses. In its most blatant form, it is often used in appeals for donations, such as: "As I have always known you to be a great supporter of our cause, I allow myself again to appeal to your generosity." Notice how just one sentence manifestly exploits praise, manipulation of self-image and the consistency tactic.

USE OTHERS TO GIVE WEIGHT TO YOUR TEXT

We are all familiar with the letter that comes to us from a colleague, co-signed by a senior executive of the company. We are equally familiar with the e-mail from a colleague addressed to several people, copied to the CEO. These are rather unsophisticated attempts at using social pressure and authority to make us respond. The writer assumes that the visible endorsement by a recognized senior person will stimulate the readers to respond. These attempts may impress us, or they may fail to do so.

There are more subtle ways of using social pressure and authority in business texts. Remember that the purpose of a business text is to evoke a response from your readers. You can increase the likelihood of getting a response by pointing out to your readers that many other people have already responded. Cialdini shows that we look at what others are doing to decide how we should behave, in particular if we believe these others to be similar to ourselves. By the same token, Thaler explains that in many situations it may be sufficient to inform people about what others are doing to nudge them into a change of behavior.

Imagine that you would like to organize a roundtable with several potential customers to discuss how your company could better serve them in the future. Suppose that you don't know these people well, and you suspect some of them may even find your invitation slightly suspect. In such situations, social pressure is most effective. Cialdini observes that we take the actions of others as a guide for our own behavior, especially in ambiguous situations. Therefore, in your invitation letter you could point to previous roundtables and to the large number of people who participated in them. Even more directly, you could indicate that several customers have already accepted the invitation to the forthcoming roundtable.

One obvious further step is to rely on the authority of a third person. If we see a recognized authority do something, we take that as a cue for correct behavior for ourselves. For example, in your invitation letter for the roundtable, you could state: "My CEO suggested that I invite you, as you are a prominent representative of the ABC region." Instead of "My CEO" you could use "Professor Zweistein." Even if your readers have never heard of Zweistein and have no clue about his contribution, the very symbol of authority may nudge them into accepting your invitation. Cialdini observes that the symbols of authority may be as convincing as the substance of authority.

Of course, the above tactics require that you do your homework before you start writing. For example, you cannot mention Zweistein if you have not spoken to him first.

CUT YOUR BROADCASTS INTO DISCRETE PERSONALIZED MESSAGES

Let's go back to the example of the monthly company newsletter you have been tasked to produce. When you send your request for news to your contact people in the various departments, you have two options: you can try to be efficient and send a standard text to your contact people as a group, or you can send a personalized text to each of them separately.

The first option may lead to what is known in social psychology as the "bystander effect". Individuals are less likely to offer help to a person in distress (e.g. the victim of a road accident) when other people are present. The greater the number of bystanders, the less likely it is that any one of them will help. As applied to your request for news, the bystander effect means that you don't get a response from anybody. Two forces lead to this effect. The first is known as "diffusion of responsibility" – each of your correspondents reasons that others will respond and therefore he can refrain from it. The second force is that of "social proof" – each of your correspondents waits for a response from the others to find out whether this request is really that serious or important.

The second option – sending a personalized text to each of your correspondents separately – should counteract both forces. You can start with the same standard text and add something *visibly* personalized. Instead of writing: "Dear correspondent, please send me a few lines about major events that took place in your department last month," you could write: "Dear Jeff, please send me a few lines about major events that took place in the Transport department last month. The Drivers' Day would be a great example." The second option doesn't take much more time or effort from you than the first option – it just requires some thoughtfulness and nine more words.

EMPHASIZE TO YOUR READERS THAT THEY WILL GET SOMETHING SCARCE

We all regularly receive leaflets with an invitation to register for a conference, stating that "the number of places is limited – places are assigned on a first-come basis." While of course we ourselves do not succumb to such a blatantly transparent trick, we suspect that many other people do. Probably they do indeed, because otherwise conference organizers wouldn't use it over and over again. The trick reveals people's fatal attraction to scarcity. The more the supply of something is limited, the more it appears valuable and desirable. Cialdini specifies that we want an item even more when it has become scarce recently and when we are competing for it with others. Furthermore, we often find more pleasure in getting something scarce than in actually using it afterwards.

You can apply the scarcity principle in your texts to evoke a response from your reader. First, you could combine the scarcity and reciprocity principle by including in your text a piece of information of which you can say to your reader that he is the first or only person with whom you share it. Even if he doesn't need the piece of information, you count on him enjoying the possession of something scarce and on his feeling of indebtedness toward you.

The second way to apply the scarcity principle is to relate scarcity to the outcome of the response you want to evoke from your reader. You could hint to your reader that he will forfeit a unique opportunity unless he responds. He should respond, not merely because you asked him to but because he will be uniquely better off. Let's go back to the example of the roundtable with your customers. In your invitation you could include: "We are organizing the roundtable only once a year and after careful selection, making sure that no direct competitors of our invitees our present. I am sure that you will find the event very informative."

EMPHASIZE TO YOUR READERS THEIR LOSS FROM FAILING TO RESPOND

The last tactic to provoke action from your readers is to appeal to their loss aversion. It is the mirror image of the previous tactic about scarcity. Instead of pointing to the unique gain the reader will enjoy from acting, you stress the loss she will suffer from inaction. Thaler explains that the feeling of hurt from losing something is twice as big as the feeling of happiness from obtaining the same thing.

You should interpret "loss" in the direct sense here, as a dispossession, not as a lost opportunity. You should indicate to your reader that, if she fails to act, she will no longer have something that she did possess, not that she will not have what she could have acquired. In other words, related to the roundtable invitation example, you could say that "your participation will ensure that you will stay on our preferred customers list," rather than "your participation will enable you to be on our preferred customers list."

FORCE A RESPONSE FROM YOUR READERS

Finally, once you have mentally persuaded your readers to act, you still have to persuade them to provide you with an answer. Don't leave your text open-ended but explicitly describe the response (or at least a couple of alternative responses) you expect. You have to force your readers to respond. Be explicit and give them a precise reason why they should respond. Cialdini points out that people respond more easily to a request for a favor if we provide them with a reason.

Remember that not responding is often an easier alternative. You don't have to be a diehard cynic to assume that business people, when not busy – which occasionally happens – are tempted by laziness. In other instances, readers prefer not to respond because they don't want to take a position or don't really have an answer. So do not give them any opportunity to escape unscathed and unburdened. Make clear the response you expect, and make it easy to act upon. You can help them by using some classic tricks like: "Unless I hear from you by that date, I will assume that you agree with my recommendation."

More generally you should provide your readers with a default option. You should indicate what you assume to be their response unless they explicitly give you another response. By doing so, you make life easy for your readers. While talking about the design of an effective choice architecture, Thaler observes that people are inclined to choose the status quo or default option that is presented to them, even if that option is not good for them. What explains the immense power of defaults is that people often are not willing or capable of spending much effort on studying other options. The choice for the default option is hardest to resist if accompanied by the suggestion that it is the normal or even recommended choice.

If there is no obvious or easy default option, you can explicitly tell your readers that you expect a response, and you can ask them to let you know what they intend to do, by when, and how. Thaler explains that the mere fact of asking people what they intend to do acts as a nudge. They are more likely to act as they said.

Imagine that you are the manager of a landscape office operating in a hotdesking mode. One of the physical laws of office life seems to be that, despite regular pleas for orderliness, people after a while leave stuff on the desk they have used. So once more you are writing a memo urging people to heed the hotdesking instructions and put things away. In your memo you could play the soft guy ("I count on your sense of good office citizenship and ask you to put your documents away") or the tough guy ("I have instructed the cleaning personnel to bin any documents left on the desks after close of business"). Neither choice promises to be very effective for you. While it is no guarantee of success (physical laws are, well, physical), you could try the following nudge: "At the bottom of this memo is a tear-off response card, where you can indicate by when and where you will put away the documents left on the desks. Please return the response card to me by tomorrow afternoon."

STAND OUT FROM THE CROWD AND GET NOTICED

In summary, don't assume that your readers will automatically attach the same importance to your text as you do. Your vitally important message may simply be a *fait divers* for them. While you have been brooding about how best to formulate your text for days, they may scan it like a page of classified ads, unlikely to register the contents unless you offer exactly what they are looking for. In most situations, your text will be competing for attention with many others. So you must make it compelling and different from the rest.

The effort it takes to stand out from the crowd depends on two factors (see Exhibit 4). First, who lies at the basis of the text? If you have been asked to write it and your offering meets a defined purpose, you will have a head start in this race. If your piece is unsolicited, you will have to work much harder to get noticed. Second, how important is the text subject to your readers? If you are addressing the professional heartland of your readers, your message will get noticed easily whereas it will take insight and stealth to sell a peripheral subject to them.

Exhibit 4: Effort required to make your text stand out

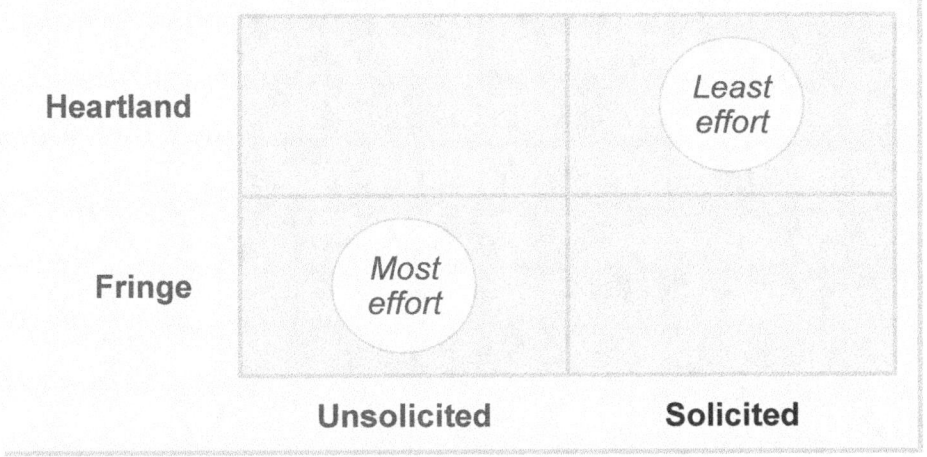

42

4

Take Into Account The Mode Of Consumption

The purpose of writing a business text is to lead your readers to act. Whether your readers will act – preferably according to your intent – depends not only on the content and form of your text, but also on the time and place at which they will consume it (see Exhibit 5). The very same text read by the very same reader with the very same prior knowledge may lead either to action exactly as you intended or to no action at all, depending on whether the text reaches him at an auspicious or inauspicious time and place.

Exhibit 5: Factors determining the readers' response to a text

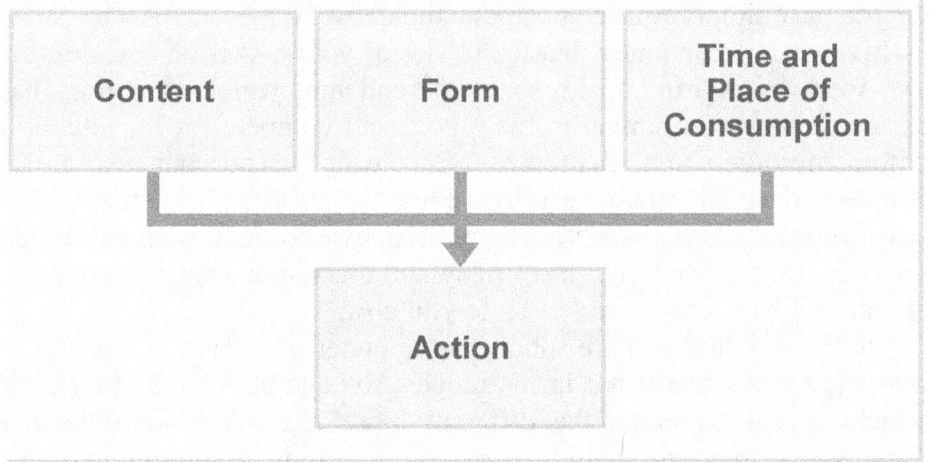

DELIVER YOUR TEXT AT A FAVORABLE TIME AND PLACE

Businesspeople are busy most of the time. Occasionally they are also grumpy. You want your text to reach them when they are most likely to be willing to free the time to read it, and to do so in a not-less-than neutral mood. It's a caricature, but it is not a terribly good idea to send a message to your boss asking for a day off three months hence, after he has spent long hours unsuccessfully negotiating with a union delegation about a new collective labor agreement and is due to resume talks after a short night's sleep. Your request may be perfectly reasonable, eloquently worked out and a model of anticipation, but you're likely to get charged with some nasty debits on that most precious of balance sheets in corporate social life, namely goodwill.

When writing and delivering a text, take into account how your readers are likely to consume it in terms of time and place. Depending on the outcome of that analysis, you may have to modify the content, form and delivery of your text. For example, if your boss is on a one-week intensive trip to another continent with only cursory access to e-mail, you may want to shorten your urgent message, just adding the sentence that a full report will await her when she's back. Or you may want to print your text on paper and hand-deliver it to the boss's assistant together with some kindly spoken delivery guideline for her. Or you may simply want to postpone the delivery.

Likewise, if you know that the reader of your text is on vacation for two weeks, it doesn't make sense to send him your text during that period. It may rest unread in his inbox, and compete for his attention with many others upon his return. Better wait to send your text until a couple of days after his return. You could even add a phrase that makes your considerate approach visible, without overdoing it, such as: "Since you were on vacation until last Friday and this memo deserves your full attention, I have chosen to send it to you now."

Or imagine that you are submitting a tender document to a prospective client, who has listed in his request for quotations the criteria by which he will compare the different bids. The addition of the list implies that bidders should structure their bids according to these criteria. After thoroughly studying the situation, you may nevertheless reason that some of the listed criteria are meaningless or duplicative. Therefore, you may decide to develop your sales pitch according to a different and more logical structure, which may also allow a better display of your company's considerable strengths. Even if, objectively speaking, your structure is indeed better, it may be unwise for you to deviate from the structure implied by the client. Just think of who will read your bid at what time and place. There may be five bids, each counting one hundred pages, to be read by a selection committee of five people, several of whom may know the tender subject only remotely or partially. They may have to do the reading of the bids on top of their other daily chores, in a rush before a deadline, without excessive zeal, using a scoring template listing the same criteria as in the request for quotation. So make their life easy and increase your chances by sticking to the structure implied by the criteria.

AS A WRITER BEHAVE AS A DESIGNER

The examples in this and previous chapters indicate that a good business writer is neither an artist nor an engineer. A good business writer is a designer. A designer envisions how people would want to use the object he has in mind, and then engineers toward that insight. He observes or imagines what people want and need, and then matches these wants or needs with what is technologically feasible. He doesn't just put an aesthetically appealing packaging around an already created object – he starts much earlier, creating ideas that better respond to people's wants and needs. While doing so, a good designer, unlike a bad engineer, ensures that his design appeals both functionally and emotionally to the targeted users. The object does the job it is intended to do *and* has an emotionally touching form and appearance.

When you write a business text, think and behave as a designer. Visualize how, where and when your reader will receive and hopefully read your text. Make sure that content, form and time and place of consumption conspire to make your text functionally and emotionally alluring.

We don't have to spend many further words on the topic of "auspicious time and place." The conclusion is straightforward: put yourself into the shoes of your reader, and think through when and where your text should best reach him to maximize its impact for you. It doesn't take much effort to do so – maybe a quick call to an assistant or another colleague. It simply takes some thoughtfulness.

5

Use Form To Your Advantage

When you write a business text, you want to evoke action from your readers. Clearly, to achieve that purpose, the logic and content of your text are the foundation. But the text form that puts your logic and content into shape has a determining influence on whether your text is noticed, taken in, read to the end, understood, interpreted correctly and acted upon by your readers according to your intent.

"Form" has three components: structure, visual appearance and technical finish (see Exhibit 6). Structure refers to the hierarchy and sequence of the content building blocks – essentially the individual paragraphs containing the arguments. Visual appearance refers to the lay-out and formatting of the text, as affected by the use of headings, fonts, colors, print features (recto verso, etc.), visuals, etc. Technical finish refers to the often mundane information that is not part of the text content as such yet aids the accessibility and acceptance of the text by its readers. Depending on the nature of the text, this can relate to such elements as page numbers, text creation date, text version number, author name, the company logo of your readers, reference number of a previous document to which the text refers and table of contents.

USE FORM TO SIGNAL QUALITY AND RESPECT

Form is important for various reasons. First there is human psychology. Most readers are no fools. They know that attractive form is no guarantee of the quality of the content of the text. But in the mind of most readers, unattractive form bodes badly for the quality of the content. If the author didn't even bother about formal quality, in all likelihood he didn't bother about the quality of the content either, the unconscious reasoning often goes.

Furthermore, many readers regard well-kempt form as a sign of respect by the author toward them. By the same token, they are prone to confer respect on the author who has made the effort to present his text well. It's like the dress-code at a party: you can either discard it as an annoying social convention or espouse it as a civilized expression of deference toward the host. In the former case, you had better be someone truly incomparable in order not to be disregarded, discredited or disparaged by the other party-goers.

Exhibit 6: The three components of "form"

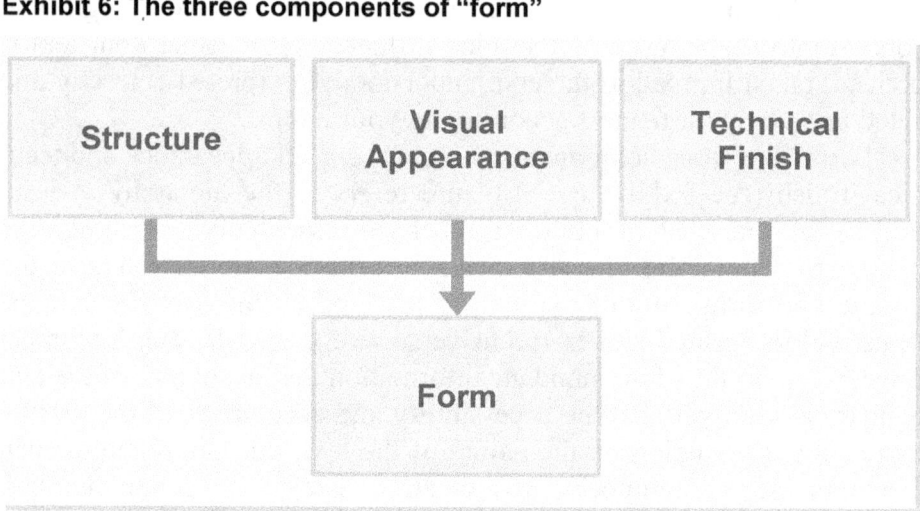

You could also make the analogy with sales reps. There must be a good reason why they usually are well dressed. Form impacts first impression, and a first impression tends to be hard to overturn. It is also true for a text. That doesn't mean, however, that you should give your text an extravagant look. Too many bells and whistles raise the reader's suspicion about the author's motives or the consequences for him. Is the author trying to dazzle or trick me into something? Is he hiding poor content or bad news? Has he got his priorities right? Doesn't he have too much time on his hands? You don't want these questions to be pertinent.

Professional sobriety is what you should aim for as far as form is concerned. The definition thereof depends on the nature and purpose of your text, as well as on the often culturally determined expectations of your readers. What may appear passionate and self-confident in one culture may appear infantile and arrogant in another.

USE FORM TO BE READER-FRIENDLY

The second reason for the importance of form is reader-friendliness. Form is an instrument for escaping from the following dilemma. On the one hand, a text needs to contain all the arguments required to convince its readers, and therefore may have to be of considerable length. A long text may also signal thoroughness and quality. On the other hand, most readers have neither the time nor the desire to go over a lengthy text. In most cases they don't even really want to dispute the content or argue with the author. They want to be convinced genuinely and quickly, so that they can move on to the next item in their mental pipeline. Therefore, the more the author helps them convince themselves in an efficient way, the more grateful they will be. Edison was probably right when he said: "There is no expedient to which a man will not go to avoid the labor of thinking."

That is where form comes into play. A well structured and visually well organized text facilitates both skimming the text and understanding its underlying logic, without feeling short-changed. Furthermore, the reader will more easily remember what he has read. And if he wants to remind himself of the content later, a quick re-read will be both possible and sufficient.

USE FORM TO ADDRESS DIFFERENT SEGMENTS SIMULTANEOUSLY

The third reason for the importance of form relates to the segmentation of your audience. As we have seen before, a text in many instances addresses various segments in its audience. Each segment may look for particular pieces of content, and consume the text at a particular time and place. Form allows the satisfaction of the needs of the various segments with one and the same text. For example, you can use side texts or attachments to address the need of one particular segment without burdening the others. Or the judicious use of bold sentences or summary paragraphs allows appreciation of the text by both the cursory and the scrupulous reader.

One peculiar segment is the so-called mosquito segment. We are all familiar with it: the people who attend a presentation and immediately turn to the pages with a pie chart to check that the percentages add up to one hundred; or those who have a fixation with bulleted lists and raise their finger to say: "I know it is not essential, but the recommendations on that list don't all start with a verb." Mosquitoes are neither lethal nor value-adding, but they are quite distracting and annoying. Don't give them a chance. Use form in general and technical finish in particular as a mosquito net for the protection of the content. The mosquitoes won't disappear, but they won't get at you any longer. For example, as befits the situation, make sure that your paper has a table of contents, that your client's name is spelled correctly on the cover page of your presentation, or that your commercial proposal carries a version number.

Finally, don't forget that there is always a chance that your audience comprises some maligned people who for reasons good or bad oppose the message in your text, and will take advantage of the comments made by the nitpickers to stage an attack against you. Don't put yourself at a disadvantage so voluntarily.

USE FORM TO SPOT SHORTCOMINGS IN LOGIC

The final reason for the importance of form relates to logic. While content should inform form, form can help reform content: as you seek out the most effective form for your text, you may spot shortcomings in the logic of your text. For example, as you are adding a cycle diagram to illustrate some reasoning, you may notice that an argument is missing in your logic. As you are identifying in a bulleted list of statements the key words that you want to put in bold, you may find that the key idea in some of these is not clear. Or, as you are revisiting your text in order to organize it into chapters, you may come across duplicated arguments to cut out, thus leading to a shorter text.

Consider, for example, the following sentence: "The pharmaceutical industry is facing strong headwinds with blockbuster patents ending, generic promotion by authorities, lowering research efficiency, fragmenting of disease cures, shrinking healthcare budgets, rising regulatory constraints, new technologies and biotechnology changing the rules of the game, and emerging countries grabbing an increasing slice of the cake." While at first sight there isn't anything intrinsically wrong with the content of the sentence, form-wise the long list of undifferentiated factors is not very appealing. As you arrange them into a bulleted list and highlight the key ideas, you notice that also content-wise the sentence is shoddy: some of the factors are related, others are hard to understand and still others don't belong in the list. A better sentence would be: "The pharmaceutical industry is facing strong headwinds: 1. Patents on blockbuster drugs are expiring while the efficiency of *research* into new drugs is declining; 2. *Regulators* are demanding more evidence about the safety and efficacy of a new drug before approving it; 3. The patient *population* is fragmenting into ever-smaller segments, as unmet needs are becoming more specific, making it harder to recoup R&D investments; 4. Healthcare *budgets* are under pressure, which leads public authorities and health insurers to implement a variety of cost-containment measures; 5. New *technologies*, while presenting the opportunity to create better treatments, are complicating the rules of the game for established companies."

BEWARE OF FORM TRANSFORMATIONS

When working on the form of your text, take into account how your readers will receive it. For example, a carefully considered bulleted list you make in an e-mail text may get transformed into a bland sequence of sentences on the reader's screen simply because her e-mail program does not recognize bullets. Variants on that theme relate to differences in paper size, printer fonts, etc. If you used form to get the content of your message across, and one way or the other the form gets corrupted, your content may get diluted. Remember: ice cream lollipops don't travel well in a backpack.

Attending to form is like taking care of personal hygiene. For the majority of gentlemen among us, the daily morning shave is a tedious chore, but after we have done it, we feel pretty good, and so most likely will the people with whom we will interact during the day.

6

Work And Work Again On Your Text

There is no escape. Writing a high-quality text takes effort and consequently time. If that sounds like bad news, here are two pieces of good news. First, it takes only a little extra effort to raise the quality of your text to a significantly higher level, provided you set your mind to it and heed the techniques explained in this book. Second, and with the same provisos, good writing follows a learning curve: as you accumulate experience, your productivity will increase.

LOOK AT GOOD WRITING AS AN INVESTMENT IN TIME

Let's take an extreme example. Assume it takes you two minutes to write an ordinary e-mail. Imagine you take double or even triple the time (my goodness, that is four or six minutes!) to write the same e-mail, yet this time of high quality. Chances are that your audience will notice, read, understand, correctly interpret and act upon your message, without you having to remind them, detail your message in a second iteration or correct their response. All in all, the total return on your extra time investment may well be higher than if you had stuck to the two-minute e-mail.

The effort put into writing a high-quality text obviously bears a relationship to its context and purpose. An e-mail to a couple of colleagues with an invitation to a house-warming party ordinarily will not merit the same ardor as a presentation to the board with an investment proposal for a power plant in Uzbekistan. High-quality writing is not an end in itself, but a means to running business more efficiently.

GRILL YOURSELF ON THE MEANING OF WHAT YOU WRITE

As you work and re-work your text, constantly ask yourself: what do I really mean, and how can I assure that my readers get the same meaning out of my writing? While answering those questions, you have to be unforgiving with yourself about the clarity of the logic and the precision of the wording you use in your text (see Exhibit 7). Fight against the seduction of intellectual laziness. Ban sloppiness in your thinking. Remember what Edison said: "Genius is one percent inspiration, ninety-nine percent perspiration."

Exhibit 7: Creating and conveying unambiguous meaning

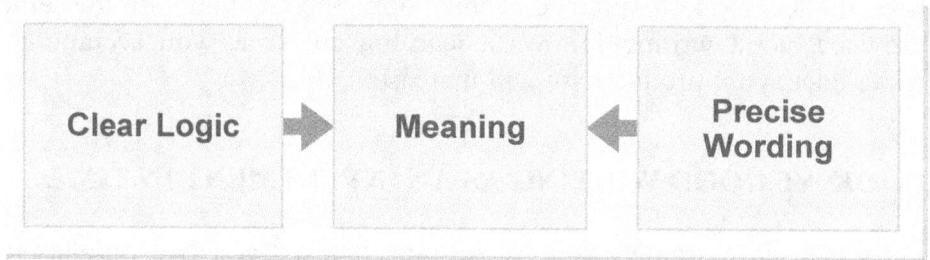

Writing is a craft. Like a sculptor working a stone, the author of a business text has to carve, chisel and polish her text until it stands as it should. That includes, by the way, re-reading a finished text – even if it is merely a perfunctory e-mail – before sending it off.

BE BUSINESS-LIKE IN BUSINESS TEXTS

Keep in mind that the purpose of a business text is to lead your readers to reasoned action. It is not to write literature let alone produce a work of art. Do not attempt to show off through the use of bizarre words or convoluted phrases just for the sake of it. At best this will slow down the speed at which your readers will understand your message. Worse, readers will accuse you of putting up a smoke screen around faulty logic – an accusation that may not be entirely untrue.

By the same token, don't gratuitously play the smart ass in your text. Always assume there will be a smarter ass than yourself in your audience, and if you ostentatiously play the smart ass, you risk provoking him into outsmarting you. Such a game may sometimes be fun, but usually it is inefficient if not annoying for the onlookers.

Be consistent in your wording. Don't use synonyms if you actually mean the same thing. If you mean "benefit", don't refer to that benefit further on with the term "advantage", "help", "gain", or any other synonym you fancy. Both you and your readers will benefit from the absence of ambiguity and the resultant efficiency gain.

GUARD AGAINST INTELLECTUAL AUTARKY

As you work and re-work your text, guard against self-inflicted mental incarceration, alternatively called intellectual autarky. It is human tendency to build walls around the fruits of one's own work. The more you have worked on your text, the more you feel you have exhausted all possible arguments, and the more you become selective and defensive. Fresh arguments crop up in your mind yet you tend to disregard them because they may upend your carefully constructed logic. Likewise, when a third party reads your draft text, you tend to disallow valuable arguments that he may bring because it would require you to reorder your thinking.

Such a posture may reflect what Cialdini calls our obsession with being consistent with what we have already done. It may also be inspired by the reluctance to admit to wasted effort: "I have already invested so much time in writing this text that I am not going to change course now." As any student of financial investment theory will tell you: "Too bad, but those are sunk costs. If you care about return on investment, you should look forward."

You may also fear the collapsing house-of-cards phenomenon: if you change one thing, the whole construction may collapse, leaving you empty-handed. Through such mental incarceration, you deny yourself the opportunity to turn a good text into a great one.

What often helps is to let your text rest for a while, and re-visit it with a fresh mind. If you do seek a review of your text by a third party, it helps to plan the review ahead of time and before you have finalized the text.

7

Put The Insights Together

Let's put together the insights from the previous chapters. You have learnt that setting your mind to creating a high-quality text is about acknowledging the following:

- The purpose of a text is to lead your readers to take reasoned action according to your intent.

- Your readers will act according to your intent only if they find meaning in your text.

- Whether your readers find meaning in your text depends, first and foremost, on its content but also on its form and its time and place of consumption.

- The quality of the content of your text depends on the clarity of the logic and the precision of the wording.

- By aligning content, form and time and place of consumption of your text, you can strengthen its meaning.

Exhibit 8 sums up what the executive action writer keeps in mind when writing a text. Memorize the scheme and visualize it whenever you are writing a text. At such a time, lean back – the imaginary cup of tea in your hands – and consider what you want to achieve, then put yourself in the position of your reader and give free rein to your creativity.

Furthermore, differentiate all of the above by reader segment: the desired action, the experienced meaning, the relevant content, the appropriate form and the suitable time and place of consumption.

Keep in mind that most people don't like to or don't have the time to read. You have to fight for their attention. And the eventual result will depend on the passion with which you go about both familiarizing yourself with the subject of your text and committing to the act of writing it. If that sounds like painful, consider another quote from

Edison: "Opportunity is missed by most people because it is dressed in overalls and looks like work."

Exhibit 8: The mental process of the Executive Action Writer

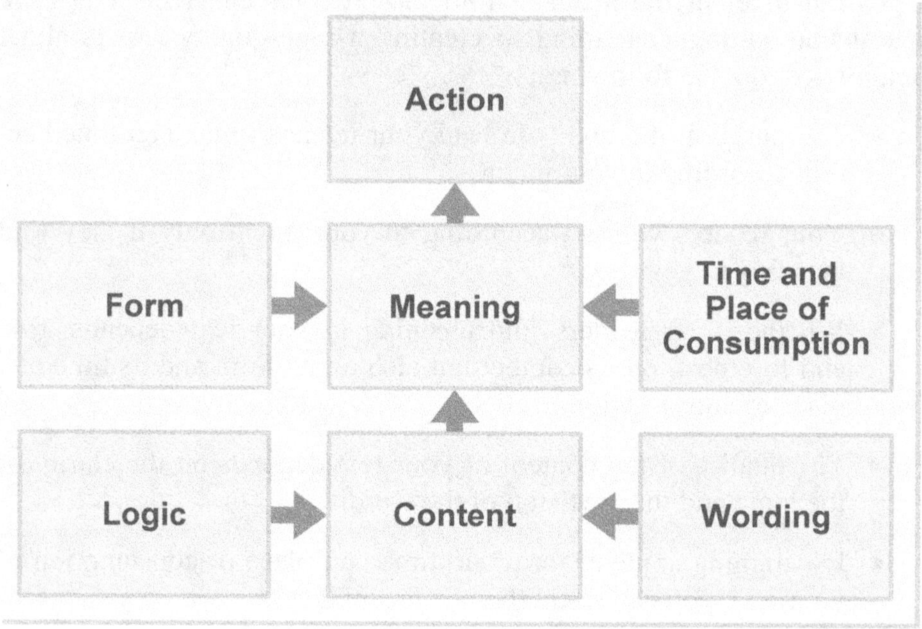

	Action	
Form →	Meaning	← Time and Place of Consumption
Logic →	Content	← Wording

Part B

CRAFT YOUR TEXT

In part A, we talked about the mindset with which to commit to the act of writing a high-quality text. We described a number of reflexes you should have when crafting a text, at least if you want it to lead your audience into acting as you intend. Table 2 summarizes the six questions that embody these reflexes. As you write a text, ask yourself these questions. If you can answer them positively, the chances are pretty strong that you will deliver a high-quality text.

Table 2: The six Executive Action Writer's questions

- Do I know enough about the subject I am writing about to produce a logical text that will convince my readers?
- Have I segmented my audience (who will or may read my text, now and in the future), and have I thought through which messages may be harmful if read by any of these segments?
- Have I made sure – through the packaging, length, lead-in, form and conclusion of my text – that it will stand out from the noise, and that my readers will pigeonhole it in the "read and act now" category?
- Have I made sure that my text will reach my readers for consumption at an auspicious time and place?
- Have I given my text the structure, visual appearance and technical finish required to make a good first impression, enable the various segments in the audience to assimilate its content in a reader-friendly way, and neutralize the nit-pickers?
- Have I used clear logic and precise wording so that my readers get the same meaning from my text as I put in?

In the second part of this book, we will give a number of examples of "original texts" that are not of high quality. By confronting them with the questions in the above table, we will show how they can be transformed into high-quality texts.

The purpose of this exercise is not to bask in the glorious comfort of hindsight, and make cheap, scathing comments about the original texts, let alone about the skills of their authors. Neither are we foolish enough to purport that the suggested alternative texts are even close to perfection. The sole purpose is to learn from confrontation.

We have modified the names of companies and people and, where needed, descriptions of subjects in order to avoid traceability of texts to companies and individuals. But otherwise we have not tinkered with the original texts.

Given the format of a book like this, we have included short examples only. For example, we have not included a PowerPoint presentation. But the principles are equally applicable to such longer texts.

The five examples that follow are not meant to be collectively exhaustive. Together they do not span the full spectrum of texts you may encounter. Neither are the suggestions for alternative texts meant to serve as models or templates that you can re-use. Their only purpose is to illustrate how a writer can drastically improve the impact of his text if he puts his mind to it.

8

Grab The Attention

The text in this example is an e-mail sent by Sean Woods, an employee working at a large global company, to seven colleagues in different regions of the world. Sean asks each of these colleagues a question about the region in which that person works. For example, to David Black, who works in Otherland, he asks a question about Otherland. Sean doesn't know any of these colleagues personally. It is the first time the colleagues, who are all much more senior than Sean, hear about the subject raised by the e-mail.

To: David Black
From: Sean Woods
Subject: Creativity and Innovation Study

Dear David,

Our company has been engaged as the Prime Knowledge Partner of the Cregio Creativity Bureau in the organisation of the 2009 Global Symposium on Creativity (www.ccb.bv).

An important aspect of our contribution to the Global Symposium is the execution of an international study of clever practices regarding economic, innovative and creative development in five different regions of the world. We will assess to what extent selected clever practices may be applicable to the partner regions of the Creative Regions network. Otherland is one of the partner regions to Cregio. The possible application of selected clever practices to Otherland is discussed in the study. An excerpt of the study concerning Otherland is added as attachment. The application is discussed in: *"Expected benefits of application"*

Since we lack 'local, specialised' knowledge of the region we would like to ask you (or another employee in your office) whether you can briefly describe to us what the main bottlenecks can be to applying the clever practices as described in the excerpt?

An example of a clever practice and a potential hurdle is noted below (First clever practice, then potential hurdle):

A good practice for Cregio is the Novel Media practice from Otherprovince. Key to its success is the "daringness to focus" thereby choosing to focus on video gaming rather than, for example, film documentaries.

A key hurdle to applying this practice in Cregio could be:
- *The inability to make this choice due to fragmented decision-making responsibilities and authority in government which may lead to less than ideal compromises.*

We would like to thank you in advance,

Kind regards,

Sean Woods

If you don't have a clue what the author of the above e-mail means, you are in the same situation as the people to whom it was sent. They didn't know any more about the subject or the author than you do.

Let's use the six Executive Action Writer's questions to make a critical assessment of the quality of this text. Each time we will give a score from 1 to 4 where: 1 = Not addressed, 2 = Poorly addressed, 3 = Acceptably addressed, 4 = Exemplary.

Question	1 Not addressed	2 Poorly addressed	3 Acceptably addressed	4 Exemplary
1. Do I know enough about the subject I am writing about to produce a logical text that will convince my readers?			☑	
2. Have I segmented my audience (who will or may read my text, now and in the future), and have I thought through which messages may be harmful if read by any of these segments?			☑	
3. Have I made sure – through the packaging, length, lead-in, form and conclusion of my text – that it will stand out from the noise, and that my readers will pigeonhole it in the "read and act now" category?	☑			
4. Have I made sure that my text will reach my readers for consumption at an auspicious time and place?		☑		
5. Have I given my text the structure, visual appearance and technical finish required to make a good first impression, enable the various segments in the audience to assimilate its content in a reader-friendly way, and neutralize the nit-pickers?		☑		

6. Have I used clear logic and precise wording so that my readers get the same meaning from my text as I put in?	☑		

The poor quality of the text is not the result of the author's lack of knowledge of the subject he is writing about. On the contrary, he has probably immersed himself so deeply in the subject that he automatically and wrongly assumes that the readers he addresses have the same level of understanding as he does.

Likewise, the poor quality of the text is not the result of insufficient segmentation of the audience or the presence of harmful messages. In fact, the author acknowledges the heterogeneity of his audience by sending separate, individually addressed mails to each of the seven recipients. Each of these mails is slightly tailored: just as the mail to David Black living in Otherland refers to Otherland, the mail to Anton Reed living in Secondland refers to Secondland, etc.

But the text fails miserably in hooking the attention of the readers. The chances are high that the text gets pigeonholed straight into the "ignore and ditch" category. The reasons are varied:

- The "Subject" description is nondescript and consequently uninviting. It is neither personalized (e.g., it doesn't refer to Otherland, unlike the text itself) nor action-oriented.

- The text is rather long, with many tidbits of information that are irrelevant to the reader. And it takes ten lines before the reader knows why he has received the text to begin with, and what is expected from him.

- Even though the author knows that his colleagues don't know him, he doesn't make any attempt to make himself special and likable to them. There is no implied compliment toward them.

- The text is discouragingly complicated. With all the references to Cregio, partner regions, Otherland, Otherprovince, practices, hurdles, etc., you really have to sit down, study the text and think before you can hope to understand it. Remember that businesspeople, busy as they always are, are rarely prepared to think long when dealing with texts that are neither solicited nor related to their professional heartland.

- The reader has no incentive to respond to the request formulated in the text. There is no indication that, should he not respond, he will forgo an opportunity beneficial to him. While we ought not to suspect that most readers are cold-blooded moneymen, we cannot blame them for subliminally including "return on investment" in their pigeonholing criteria.

- Form-wise the text appears rather chaotic. The author uses sentences in bold and indents, but these do not support the content well.

- Even to the most willingly responsive reader, it is not clear how to respond meaningfully to the author's request. A clear specification of the expected response is absent from the text. Neither is it made easy to respond.

- Finally, the text does not have a closure from which it is hard to escape. There are no indications of urgency or deadline. No follow-up is foreseen, such as "I will contact you by phone …" It is not made easy for the cooperative reader to react (e.g., the author has not added his phone number). There is no teaser. There is no suggestion that the reader should delegate the task to a more knowledgeable colleague.

Of the seven colleagues, two responded without further prompting, yet with requests to Sean to clarify his expectations first. Two others responded after several reminders by Sean. A further two grudgingly responded after some verbal prodding by Sean's supervisor. One recipient did not respond at all.

If only Sean had set his mind to crafting a high-quality text from the start, a huge amount of effort would have been saved, by himself, his supervisor and his colleagues. And the responses would have been much more meaningful. The extra initial investment that would have been required from Sean? At most ten more minutes of thinking and writing – well worth it. Below is a suggested alternative text.

To: *David Black*
From: *Sean Woods*
Subject: *Business opportunity in Otherland*

Dear David,

I am scheduled to meet with several high-level representatives of Otherland at the upcoming Global Symposium on Creativity. The purpose of the meeting is to discuss the applicability – to Otherland – of the clever creativity-stimulating practices that we have identified in a worldwide study of creative regions. The first draft of the text that will form the basis for that discussion is attached herewith. Given your familiarity with current practice in Otherland and my concern not to say anything that would contradict your viewpoints, I would highly appreciate it if you could review this draft (below I've detailed the specific question I have), by September 30th at the latest.

You are of course most welcome to join me at that meeting and establish a business contact with the Otherland representatives – for more details, just give me a call on +xx-xxx.xxx.xxx. If you think one of your colleagues is better suited, please forward this mail, with copy to me.

Many thanks,
Sean
Tel. +xx-xxx.xxx.xxx

****

The attached three-page text consists of three parts describing:
- A number of clever creativity-stimulating practices applied by creative regions
- The benefits that Otherland might derive from applying these practices in Otherland
- The hurdles that Otherland should overcome before it can apply these practices

The latter part has been left mostly empty. Could you please complete it – it will take at most fifteen minutes of your time. To make it easy for you, I have added below a table with two columns. The first column simply re-lists the benefits described in the text; the second column on hurdles is for you to fill in.

Benefits	Hurdles
Abc	*Please fill in*
Def	*Please fill in*
Ghi	*Please fill in*

We are making this study in our role as Prime Knowledge Partner of the Cregio Creativity Bureau. The study results will be presented at the 2009 Global Symposium on Creativity (www.ccb.bv). Representatives of Otherland and many other regions will participate.

9

Address All Segments

The text in this example is a speech at a farewell party for Pete Nestinck, an employee at BigProject Inc. Pete received an attractive job offer from another company, ChemCorp, and was thus leaving BigProject on good terms. Pete was widely respected by his colleagues. The farewell party was an informal affair, organized as an unpretentious drink at 5pm in the company's main conference room, with some fifteen colleagues attending. It is Pete's boss, Romano Prattini, who is giving the speech.

Pete:

You joined BigProject seven years ago as a junior analyst. Initially, you spent a lot of time working on projects for clients in the consumer goods industry. And successfully so: after only two years, you got your first promotion.

At that time, your focus shifted, and you started working on projects in the telecommunications sector. Again, you used your great skill to impress clients and colleagues, which led to your next promotion.

Your reputation spread fast and far, and you were called to serve the company by working on projects in yet another sector, namely the government sector. But as if that were not enough, from time to time you ventured into still other sectors, not the least into pharmaceuticals.

This diversity points to the first of the capabilities you possess and from which we have been able to benefit in this company: your versatility. And versatility is important to run this company profitably.

The second capability that we admire in you are your smarts. But above all, your smarts coupled with modesty. Even when you are head and shoulders above your peers, yourself you stay modest.

Last but not least, I should point to your knack of dealing with the most difficult clients. Whenever we had a difficult client, we knew we could put you in charge, and you would mellow them. A great gift!

So, it is nothing but natural that we regret your leaving us. And I must admit your decision came a bit as a surprise. Because as far as I can tell, impatience or rashness are none of your traits. But now that you've made that decision, I wish you the very best, and I am very sure you will do very well indeed in your new job. The things that served you well here – integrity, good humor, positive attitude, listening skills and discretion – will also serve you well in your new job at ChemCorp.

And should it be such that you get bored in your new job, don't hesitate to come knocking again at our door! Pete, thank you again for the time you spent with us. Best of luck in your new challenge, and stay in touch!

If you don't feel very tickled by listening to the above speech, you feel the same as Pete and his colleagues did.

Let's again use the six Executive Action Writer's questions to make a critical assessment of the quality of this text. Each time we will give a score from 1 to 4 where: 1 = Not addressed, 2 = Poorly addressed, 3 = Acceptably addressed, 4 = Exemplary. Of course, a speech is totally different from a text of a more factual nature. It is much more personal and often hard to appreciate by outsiders because it is packed with inside jokes and covert messages. Nevertheless, the quality of a speech text used in a business environment can be assessed in the same way as any other business text.

Question	1 Not addressed	2 Poorly addressed	3 Acceptably addressed	4 Exemplary
1. Do I know enough about the subject I am writing about to produce a logical text that will convince my readers?		☑		
2. Have I segmented my audience (who will or may read my text, now and in the future), and have I thought through which messages may be harmful if read by any of these segments?	☑			
3. Have I made sure – through the packaging, length, lead-in, form and conclusion of my text – that it will stand out from the noise, and that my readers will pigeonhole it in the "read and act now" category?		☑		
4. Have I made sure that my text will reach my readers for consumption at an auspicious time and place?			☑	
5. Have I given my text the structure, visual appearance and technical finish required to make a good first impression, enable the various segments in the audience to assimilate its content			☑	

in a reader-friendly way, and neutralize the nit-pickers?			
6. Have I used clear logic and precise wording so that my readers get the same meaning from my text as I put in?	☑		

While the above speech doesn't say anything wrong and is well structured, it just doesn't stick. The reasons are varied:

- The author apparently didn't make much effort in digging up specific bits of information about Pete. The few facts he mentions are either widely known by the audience or barely instrumental in conveying an exciting message. The story comes across as a perfunctory speech by, well, a boss. There is little display of emotion, no personal touch – the talk is always about "we" and "the company", never about "I" and "Romano Prattini."

- The author assumes his audience is a segment of one: Pete, and no one else. But in a business environment, when you give a farewell speech, you have another segment that is at least as important as the fêted person: Pete's colleagues. The author completely ignores this latter segment. He always addresses Pete, as if no one else is present in the room. He makes no effort to involve Pete's colleagues, as he could do, for example, by switching between "you, Pete" and "him, Pete." As a result, he forgoes a rare opportunity to convey messages that may be hard to convey otherwise.

- In fact, Pete's colleagues would expect that the boss does take this opportunity. Of course, a fine balance has to be struck. Tongue in cheek, you can afford – or are even expected – to say things to the colleagues you couldn't say in a different situation. At the same time, you don't want to be seen abusing this freedom of speech.

- As a consequence, this speech will lead to little action. Sure, Pete may feel reasonably good about it, and in the future talk favorably about his former employer. But will the colleagues remember the speech, let alone its author as a good speaker? Will their pride of working for BigProject be rekindled? Will they find inspiration in Pete for their own future behavior within BigProject?

In summary, to achieve its purpose, the text should be made much more concrete – there should be something in it for everybody. And, without degrading into a corny or cheesy narrative, it should be somewhat emotional and theatrical. Below is a suggested alternative text.

Pete, you're leaving – I still cannot believe it.

You know, when you came to see me to tell me that you had decided to "change career", as they say, we started chatting, and at a certain point, I asked: "Well, Pete, how long have you been with BigProject? Twelve years or so?" I won't forget your reaction. You had a terrified look in your eyes, as if I had said something very sinful. "No, no, no, no," you replied. "Only seven years!" But you see, for me it is like you have always been with BigProject. And for someone like me who has been with BigProject for 20 years, that is a very long time indeed.

I cannot imagine BigProject without you. You're one of these guys that are the bedrock – often barely visible – upon which a service organization like ours can grow in a durable way. There are several reasons for that.

First of all, Pete is versatile. He has been a guru in fast-moving consumer goods; for a while also in telecommunications; then in the public sector; finally in big pharma; and soon at ChemCorp also in, let me check, "polyalphaolefins" – whatever that means. But, as we all know, being versatile in a credible way, is important in this business.

Second, Pete is a smart guy. In fact, Pete is smarter than he thinks himself, which – trust me – is a rare gift in this profession.

But, most importantly of all, Pete is the guy you like to have in charge of projects at very difficult, if not impossible, clients – be it Birdy Smith at Piano Ltd., or Lara Croft at Jacksens. He will make them feel at ease, no matter what.

So, Pete, that is why I thought you had been with BigProject for as long as I can remember. But also if I look at the future, I really cannot imagine BigProject without you. In this business, it is normal that people come, and then go. But with most people, you know that one day they will be gone. The only

---

question is "when?" You know from their characters that one day they will be gone. For example, because they combine, how shall I say, excessive degrees of impatience with self-confidence. Or because they feel more at ease in operational positions than in jobs with a high conceptual content. But Pete? No one could accuse Pete of being impatient, excessively self-confident or short on conceptual skills. So, Pete, I still cannot believe you're leaving.

That said, I am 100 per cent sure you will do great in your new job. In fact, I guess you would do well in any job. I've done a bit of undercover journalism in the past few days, and asked people to think wildly, and imagine which profession would fit Pete best. You know what came out? I'll tell you, Pete, and don't look at me again with these terrified eyes. What came out is that you would be an excellent psychotherapist, and – dare I say – certainly so in the women's department. People praise your integrity, constant good humor, positive outlook on life, listening skills and discretion.

In other words, Pete, what I really want to say is: if you get bored with your new job selling nameless chemical molecules such as polybutenes, you can either come back to BigProject or start your psychotherapy practice. You'll be successful in both. Cheers!

10

Force A Response

The text in this example is an e-mail sent by Joyce Seafinn, the financial controller, to the heads of several business departments, requesting them to provide her with data necessary to prepare next year's budget. In fact, the text is made up of two consecutive e-mails, sent within the space of five minutes. The second e-mail adds some clarification to the first.

Friday, November 17, 2:57 pm

To: Department heads
From: Joyce Seafinn
Subject: Product line sales forecasts

Hello,

I need your input in the attached Excel table that constitutes one of the elements of the budget exercise for next year.

Thanks in advance for completing this table as well as chapter 2 of the Word file. It is a must that these documents can be discussed and finalised during the Management Board meeting this Monday. Thanks in advance for your help and sorry for asking at such short notice.

Best regards

Joyce Seafinn
Financial controller

***

Friday, November 17, 3:01 pm

To: Department heads
From: Joyce Seafinn
Subject: Product line sales forecasts

!!! I forgot to specify that you should complete one table for each country (country A and B separately).
Thanks
Best regards

Joyce Seafinn
Financial controller

Imagine you're one of the department heads to whom the above e-mails are sent. How would you react when receiving these? Unless the financial controller inspires fear or pity – either of which is not impossible – your response is likely to be minimalist at best. And that is exactly what happened: when the Management Board met on Monday, the data presented by Joyce were incomplete – and she got clobbered for it by the boss.

Let's again use the six Executive Action Writer's questions to make a critical assessment of the quality of this text. Each time we will give a score from 1 to 4 where: 1 = Not addressed, 2 = Poorly addressed, 3 = Acceptably addressed, 4 = Exemplary.

Question	1 Not addressed	2 Poorly addressed	3 Acceptably addressed	4 Exemplary
1. Do I know enough about the subject I am writing about to produce a logical text that will convince my readers?			☑	
2. Have I segmented my audience (who will or may read my text, now and in the future), and have I thought through which messages may be harmful if read by any of these segments?		☑		
3. Have I made sure – through the packaging, length, lead-in, form and conclusion of my text – that it will stand out from the noise, and that my readers will pigeonhole it in the "read and act now" category?	☑			
4. Have I made sure that my text will reach my readers for consumption at an auspicious time and place?		☑		
5. Have I given my text the structure, visual appearance and technical finish required to make a good first impression, enable the various segments in the audience to assimilate its content in a reader-friendly way, and neutralize the nit-pickers?	☑			

6. Have I used clear logic and precise wording so that my readers get the same meaning from my text as I put in?		☑	

The financial controller had formulated her e-mails in a polite way. They were also pretty unambiguous about what she was after: "Give me those bloody sales figures." If the e-mails nevertheless failed to have the intended impact, it is because they gloriously licensed the recipients to escape from responding:

- Some of the targeted department heads were resident in countries other than that of the financial controller and did not understand the language in which she had written the e-mails (French). It's a pretty basic mistake not to use the corporate language (English).

- The very fact of sending a second explanatory e-mail only minutes after the first signals that the whole request may not have been thought through very well, triggering the likely response: "Maybe she was a trifle impulsive and doesn't really need those figures after all. And who knows, maybe there will be a third e-mail with yet another instruction. Why not wait and see?"

- The mail was accompanied by two attachments. The first, a spreadsheet, was fairly straightforward. However, the second, a text document, was 15 pages long, including the request to complete chapter 2. The link between that chapter and the requested figures, and therefore its relevance, was unclear, leading to the likely response: "Maybe she made a mistake, and she meant another chapter. Better wait and see."

- The financial controller did very little to lend authority to her request. To begin with, she could have given a bit more context to her request. And she could have referred to the origin of her request: her and everybody's boss. And she could have stated that anybody who did not fully understand the request should call her.

- Finally, her timing was unfortunate. When an unclear and burdensome request lands in your inbox on Friday afternoon, the temptation to ditch it with the fake excuse that you didn't read it before the close of business may be irresistible. And that is what happened.

In summary, the text is almost completely neglectful of how it will be received by its intended audience, despite the urgency and the author's realization that she is asking something special. If only she had given a bit more thought to how she should craft the simple e-mail, she would have spared the department heads, the boss Art Dennes and herself much aggravation. Below is a suggested alternative text.

Friday, November 17, 2:57 pm

To: Department heads
From: Joyce Seafinn
Subject: Urgent – your forecasts required at 5 pm for meeting with Art Dennes

Hello,

As communicated by Art, next year's budget is on the agenda of the Management Board meeting this Monday. One of the breakdowns he wants to discuss is sales forecast by product line. Since we don't have these figures yet, he has requested that each of you provides them to me by 5 pm this afternoon.

Please use the table in the attached Excel spreadsheet. The rows list the product lines for which each of you are responsible. Please make a split between country A and country B, as indicated in the table.

You should also provide an answer to the question that is written beneath the table in the same spreadsheet. It asks for the assumptions underlying your sales forecasts. Your answers will form a chapter in the budget document that Art will have to send to Corporate afterwards.

Don't hesitate to call me on extension 746 if there is any doubt about what you need to do. If I don't hear from you, I will assume that the request is clear and that I can have your response by 5 pm today.

Many thanks for your understanding and prompt reply to this short-notice request.

Joyce Seafinn
Financial controller

11

Think Before You Write

The text in this example is an e-mail from Tim French, Corporate Human Resources (HR) Director at DoubleCokes, a multinational company with a history and culture of granting much operating autonomy to its Business Units (BUs). A new CEO, Jack Spetter, came on board a year earlier. He created the Corporate HR function and hired Tim from the outside two months before. Through the e-mail, Tim announces to all BU heads the launch of a project to introduce a web-based solution to support the company's performance management process. The e-mail is the first time the BU heads have heard about the project.

Date: March 12, 2009
To: Heads of Business Units
Cc: Jack Spetter
From: Tim French
Subject: CARE Initiative : Performance Management ++ Action required ++

Dear BU Heads,

We need to streamline and facilitate our Performance Management Process and are consequently launching a "CARE" initiative in the coming days.
"CARE" stands for "Continuous Assessment of Results and Expectations ".
"CARE" as we care about our people development
"CARE" to improve our employer brand and people loyalty and readiness.
"CARE" to reduce paper work and administration

CARE initiative will have two roads
> 1.Design our Performance Management processes , job profiles, KPI , competences, etc
> 2.Parameterise an HR Performance Management system based on the above.

We will manage both in strict parallel during the coming months in order to leverage the Process by the System and vice-versa. The HR system will be supplied by "SuperDuperHR". (SDHR)

Please, take 5 ' to read the information below and know more about the CARE project and initiative and email me by December Friday, 7 using,the attached Xls, the names of your future local CARE champions
> 1.Participant (s) to the March 22 SuccessFactors 90 ' demonstration + Q&A
> 2.CARE Key-User(s) + CARE Key-User(s) Back-up
> 3.And recommend me who could be a CARE Project team Team Member.

We will minimize the work load related to the project . Most of the users will need less than 2 hours to use efficiently our CARE system and process.

Ad hoc project codes will be communicated soon

Feel free to call me as needed.

Tim French
Corporate HR Director

Performance Management at DoubleCokes

In DoubleCokes, some Performance Management good practices and straight full processes exist but there is also a great expectation for improvement, for internal coherence as a clear need to reduce paperwork administration and time simply lost in routine.

Together with Jack Spetter, we have agreed to implement during Q2 2009 a global web based "on demand solution" supporting a Global and local Performance Management processes. By implementing existing and new good practices we will enable the measurement, alignment and achievement of our individual, local and global goals.

This on line HR application will fully support our Global CARE initiative "Continuous Assessment of Result and Expectations" such the various appraisal reviews, 360 ° feed-back, the career development aspects, the career planning and our pay-for-performance.

CARE (Continuous Assessment of Result and Expectations)

Our CARE project will have two roads
> 1.Set up our Performance Management processes , job profiles, KPI , templates etc
> 2.Parameterise an HR Performance Management system based on the above.

We will manage both in strict parallel during the coming months in order to leverage the Process by the System and vice-versa.

Starting April, the first step of our CARE project will cover the

> •Goal Management : individual, BU, Global
> •Performance appraisals
> •Career path, career planning, promotions
> •Internal Talent Search
> •Balanced scorecards, Dashboard

We expect to go-life by September, 1. From there, we will manage our entire Project Performances Reviews as well as our 2009 end-year review with this tool.

Starting Q3 and Q4, the second step of our CARE project will cover

> •Pay for performance
> •Salary decision
> •Market pricing
> •Incentive and Bonus
> •Pay- Equity or stock program

83

Our goal is to start to manage the Remuneration and Compensation process from January.

Each actor in the CARE processes work flow will be able to access any time at finger tips the relevant information such job profile, to easily give his input trough DoubleCokes templates such 360 ° appraisal, to meet the due dates and to get ad-hoc dashboard allowing him to make decision in due time.

Performance Management System

After a market review of the various Performance Management vendors and based on our actual and coming 3 year needs, our decision is to implement the SuperDuperHR on demand web based solution. You will receive in the coming days by post a CD with a first presentation. You can also access the SuperDuperHR web site. http://www.SuperDuperHR.cim/

What next ?

A critical requirement for rapid and wise CARE implementations is to assign the appropriate resources with clearly defined individual accountability.

Demonstration + Action require +

There is no limitation to the number of participants. They just need an internet connection and a telephone. You have to appoint your representatives to join one of those demos.

A 60 to 90 'life on-line demo + Q&A with a DoubleCokes scenario of the SuperDuperHR system will take place as follow
        •for Europe on line March 22, 12 am CET time
        •for US on-line March, 22 9 am local time
        •For Asia on-line March, 22 10 am CET time.

Key User + Action required +

You have to appoint your local CARE Key-User and his back-up. We recommend one Key-User by 50 users. The key-user is the local person who will be the trainer and support for all other users. He will be specifically trained.

Key-user must be available
on request once in April and for about 4 times 2 hours in June and July for testing, training and learning purpose
As needed to train and support local users in July-October should not be more than 2 to 3 hours a week.

THINK BEFORE YOU WRITE

They are typically good with people and are level N-3, N-2 or HR manager when existing.

CARE Key-Users will
- •get specific Webex or on-line training,
- •test the systems once designed by the project team,
- •cascade training sessions to the local users staff and support functions
- •Support local users during the first months after the go-live.

Most of the training session will be on-line and self-learning will be quite easy and facilitate by the on-line assistant.

Steering Committee

The Steering Committee will be in touch 5 or 6 times 2 hours to review the work done by the project team. They will validate the processes, templates and KPI and control the project critical steps including agreement for "go-life.

The members are senior managers:
1. For Europe : *TBC*
2. For US : *TBC*
3. For Asia : GS Kim
4. Jack Spetter
5. Tim French
6. SuperDuperHR Project Leader

Project team + Proposal required +

The project team will collect existing internal best practices and set up the Global Goals and Appraisal process with all related documents such job profiles, career levels, competences referential, scorecards, KPI and process mapping. Once approved by the Steering Committee they will translate this into the SuperDuperHR System and Global guidelines.

From April to June, each team member will have to dedicate about 6 to 8 days to the CARE project including home work, travel, on-line and physical meetings. This work will be part of their 2009 MBO. Team Members are experienced N-3, N-2 or N-1 or HR manager when existing.

I am welcoming any candidate but the team should be representative and not exceed 8 members. You have to recommend me some project team members out of your BU team as follow

The project team should be composed as follow

•DoubleCokes Project Leader   Tim French
•Team member   Benelux
•Team member   France
•Team member   Italy or Spain
•Team member   Central Europe
•Team member   Nordic or UK
•Team member   US
•Team member   Asia
•Team member   Asia

IT, communication, training will be involved as needed

Timing

The actual *tentative* agenda for the Goal and Appraisal bit of the project should look like as below

Demo with Key-users and Country deputies   Mid of March
Kick-off meeting with Project team: **April**
Internal preparation with the Project Team   April- May
System Parameterisation   May-June
Data loading   End of June
Key-User training: Second half of June

Go-life: July, 1
Users training   First 2 weeks of July
First Project review   **From July**
Local End-year Review: December

Communication

We are today formally introducing this CARE initiative to all of you. We will do the same to N-2 Managers by end of March and to our staff by beginning of April.

You will be in touch with the project trough your Key-users, project team-members and by several monthly including one during the April annual management meeting. You will get some brief and communication material to explain the CARE initiative during your staff meetings.

One way or one other, an intranet will be created to support our CARE project and initiative
Good and simple training opportunities and many job aids will be available.

CARE project is a good way to make our life simpler. Be sure we will follow-

> up on progress and successes.

Imagine you are one of the BU heads and get the above e-mail in your inbox. The colour of your reaction probably would depend on your personality and style. Certainly at DoubleCokes, the BU heads' reactions were diverse, but none of them embraced Tim's initiative with the slightest hint of enthusiasm. Reasoning "Respond to Tim now and he will be off my back," the most gentle among them simply yet sparsely provided Tim with some of the information he requested, i.e. the name of the person attending the demo and the key user's name. Others didn't read his mail beyond the first 20 lines and responded negatively with a message essentially saying: "What a nonsensical idea is this – haven't we got any better uses of our time and money?!" Still others ignored Tim's mail, reasoning "Live and let live – if this is really serious, we'll hear about it again." None of this is quite effective, is it?

Let's again use the six Executive Action Writer's questions to make a critical assessment of the quality of this text. Each time we will give a score from 1 to 4 where: 1 = Not addressed, 2 = Poorly addressed, 3 = Acceptably addressed, 4 = Exemplary.

Question	1 Not addressed	2 Poorly addressed	3 Acceptably addressed	4 Exemplary
1. Do I know enough about the subject I am writing about to produce a logical text that will convince my readers?	☑			
2. Have I segmented my audience (who will or may read my text, now and in the future), and have I thought through which messages may be harmful if read by any of these			☑	

segments?				
3. Have I made sure – through the packaging, length, lead-in, form and conclusion of my text – that it will stand out from the noise, and that my readers will pigeonhole it in the "read and act now" category?		☑		
4. Have I made sure that my text will reach my readers for consumption at an auspicious time and place?			☑	
5. Have I given my text the structure, visual appearance and technical finish required to make a good first impression, enable the various segments in the audience to assimilate its content in a reader-friendly way, and neutralize the nit-pickers?	☑			
6. Have I used clear logic and precise wording so that my readers get the same meaning from my text as I put in?		☑		

The above text makes no mistake about the audience it is addressing. It clearly targets the BU heads, and the BU heads rightly see themselves as the target. The subject of the text is also sufficiently weighty and timeless to make it of little relevance when and where it reaches them.

The abysmal quality of the text stems from Tim's appalling disregard of how the business works and how the BU heads operate. The text makes the BU heads ponder: "Either Tim is dumb or Tim thinks we are dumb." Both possibilities are unpalatable. Consider the thoughts the text evokes in their heads:

- It is blatant that the hoopla about CARE at the start of the text is just a smokescreen for the ultimate objective of imposing a web-based tool enabling Tim (and Jack) to get a stronger grip on day-to-day HR management within the BUs. Of course it is the prerogative of the CEO and his support staff to have this on their agenda. But then they should be open about it rather than introduce it by stealth.

- Another explanation for Tim's initiative is that as a newcomer in a corporate support job he wishes to make his mark and prove his worth to the BUs quickly. Of course that is a common and acceptable objective. But then he should go about it more smartly. For example, Tim could have enlisted a couple of opinion-leading BU heads first. It is quite ironic that such disregard of the basic rules of change management should be present in a senior HR professional.

- Whatever Tim's motive, the lousy quality of his text demonstrates a basic lack of respect for the readers. Parts of the text look like a straight copy & paste from one used at his previous employer or from SuperDuperHR's website. Of course there is nothing wrong with being smart and not re-inventing the wheel, but then he should do so judiciously. Furthermore, spelling mistakes are rampant in the text. Shouldn't one expect better of a text on such a weighty subject from corporate HR?

- Tim leaves the door wide open to the BU heads to relish their genetically disposed cynicism toward anything originating from corporate staff functions. Consider Tim's last two sentences: "CARE project is a good way to make our life simpler. Be sure we will follow-up on progress and successes." Sure.

The BU heads' thoughts may be neither fair nor effective, yet they did exist and determined their actions – or lack thereof. The CARE initiative died a stillborn death. No more was heard about it after Tim's infamous e-mail.

This situation is a prime example of the maxim "Think before you write." As a consequence, it is pretty meaningless to suggest merely textual modifications to Tim's e-mail. It is even worthwhile considering whether Tim should communicate through a broadcast message like the one he used. Since there are fewer than ten BU heads, he would do better to pick up the phone or see each of them face-to-face.

Assuming that Tim still wants to use a broadcast message, he should, first and foremost, re-think his course of action. He could gain legitimacy first by enlisting the support of a couple of opinion-leading BU heads through bilateral communication. Their support could materialize through the appointment of a team member. Afterwards Tim could organize the broadcast message to the BU heads in two steps. In the first step, he could ask the CEO, Jack Spetter, to announce the why and why now of the CARE initiative in broad terms, while referring to a subsequent message to expect from Tim. This would enable the BU heads to air any concerns about the basics of the initiative before Tim loses them through details and premature practical arrangements. In the second step he could lay out specific actions in an e-mail, referring to the BU heads who have already given their support to the initiative.

12

Display Passion

The text in this example is an e-mail about swine flu from Ben Black-smith to all staff. Ben is the Administration Manager in the local country office of a multinational company. So far swine flu had barely spread in the country, and Ben had got himself involved in the precautionary measures. He had put posters on the walls with reminders of hand hygiene, he had distributed alcohol gel disinfectants to all employees in the office and he had forwarded several mail messages about swine flu from Corporate HR. Below is the latest one. It refers to a ten-page hand-out attached to his mail.

Friday, August 21

To: All staff
From: Ben Blacksmith
Subject: Pandemic Flu - update 2

Hello

Please find herewith a hand-out issued by Corporate HR with useful information on the A/H1N1 flu.

Regards
Ben

Usually we are in favor of brevity. This text, however, is compressed beyond the limits of usefulness. It is a safe guess that half of the staff members deleted the e-mail without even opening it, and that half of the staff members who did open the e-mail then didn't bother to open and read the attachment. That cannot have been the intent.

Let's again use the six Executive Action Writer's questions to make a critical assessment of the quality of this text. Each time we will give a score from 1 to 4 where: 1 = Not addressed, 2 = Poorly addressed, 3 = Acceptably addressed, 4 = Exemplary.

Question	1 Not addressed	2 Poorly addressed	3 Acceptably addressed	4 Exemplary
1. Do I know enough about the subject I am writing about to produce a logical text that will convince my readers?	☑			
2. Have I segmented my audience (who will or may read my text, now and in the future), and have I thought through which messages may be harmful if read by any of these segments?			☑	
3. Have I made sure – through the packaging, length, lead-in, form and conclusion of my text – that it will stand out from the noise, and that my readers will pigeonhole it in the "read and act now" category?	☑			
4. Have I made sure that my text will reach my readers for consumption at an auspicious time and place?			☑	
5. Have I given my text the structure, visual appearance and technical finish required to make a good first impression, enable the various segments in the audience to assimilate its content in a reader-friendly way, and neutralize the nit-pickers?	☑			
6. Have I used clear logic and precise wording so that my readers get the same meaning from my text as I put in?		☑		

Ben's is an example of how a well intentioned text manages to get pigeonholed in the "ignore straight away" category:

- The pigeonholing process started when the targeted readers looked at their inboxes. The very combination of author name (Ben Blacksmith) and text subject (Pandemic Flu - update 2) triggered an almost automatic "delete" response. While Ben was known as a diligent administrator, he was not known as a source of insightful information. The subject title suggests neither any exciting news nor any urgent action to be taken. In fact, with this mail Ben shoots himself in the foot again. It confirms the personal brand image that his colleagues – fairly or unfairly – attach to him: "Nice guy, but not of much added value as far as I am concerned."

- The kind colleagues who did open the mail were then hit by a pretty meaningless single sentence. There is no indication of what could possibly be interesting in the attachment or what action the reader should take beyond reading it. The very fact of referring to Corporate HR in and of itself is discouraging. Ben's text leads to a variety of reactions, none of which is flattering for him or, worse, evokes action. The first reaction could be: "Personally Ben probably doesn't think the information is useful but he has got to comply with Corporate's request to distribute this. But if even he doesn't think it is useful, why should I bother?" Another reaction: "Huh, lazy Ben probably didn't even bother to read it himself – why should I?" Or: "Poor Ben. Shows again he is not capable of understanding our needs."

- The adventurous colleagues who did open the attachment were hit by ten dense pages of text that had clearly been copied from a variety of sources. Few people bothered to read it. While Ben was not responsible for the content of the attachment, he should have known that his colleagues in all likelihood were already swamped by information about swine flu prevalence, symptoms and precautions from other sources (newspapers, TV, social networking sites, etc.). He could have summarized in two lines what the hand-out was about, and he could have added a couple of practical pieces of relevant advice for his colleagues.

In summary, Ben's mail is a non-event. It is an unsolicited, peripheral message to its readers, and it breathes detachment from its author. But its opportunity cost is high, both for Ben and the company. Ben could have used it to burnish rather than tarnish his personal brand. And maybe there was some useful information in the hand-out that could have led to action with an important impact, if not immediately then at least in the future. Below is a suggested alternative text.

Friday, August 21

To: *All staff*
From: *Ben Blacksmith*
Subject: *From the flurry of information about swine flu, some practical hints for you*

Hello

We are all swamped by sometimes contradictory information from various sources about the novel influenza A/H1N1, commonly known as swine flu. Please find herewith a hand-out that summarizes well the latest information about its prevalence, symptoms, precautions and treatment.

If you are already well informed, here are nevertheless two practical tips:

- Copy the URL of the US Centers for Disease Control and Prevention (www.cdc.gov) into your BlackBerry. It provides up-to-date information, including about places to which you may be travelling.

- Attend one of the free walk-in training sessions that our neighbourhood hospital is organizing about when and how to use masks correctly. The list of dates is available in my office.

If you have further questions, please come and see me.

Regards
Ben

Epilogue

Businesses are increasingly knowledge-intensive, open, networked and global. Management decision-making is becoming more complex and fast-paced. Traditional hierarchical command and control lines are losing their potency. The force of goodwill and the power of persuasion are driving what really does or does not happen in day-to-day business. Accordingly communication has become the lubricant of today's business world. Effective communications, verbal and written, determine whether things move or don't. So it is vitally important for businesspeople to write effective texts.

This is common sense, yet not common practice. Many business texts fail to persuade the reader to take the action required. They are ignored, misunderstood or misinterpreted. They lead to aggravation and waste. They make business inefficient.

The purpose of this book is to advise businesspeople how to craft texts that will evoke the response they want from their target audience. I hope that I have succeeded in convincing you that writing a high-quality business text is a matter not so much of technical perfection as of mindset. Whenever you are about to write a text, allow yourself first to relax and think. Lean back – the imaginary cup of tea in your hands – and consider what you want to achieve, then put yourself in the position of your reader and give free rein to your creativity. That is what *The Executive Action Writer* is all about.

On other occasions, you may not be the writer but the reader of a business text. If you feel the slightest temptation to do anything other than pigeonhole that text in the "read and act now" category, at least you could return the text to its writer with the advice to read this very book. And I am only half-joking.

Alternatively you are most welcome to send original examples of poor-quality texts to me at herman@teawriter.com, together with your observations, insights or recommendations. I may find inspiration in these for, who knows, a revised edition of *The Executive Action Writer*.

Bibliography

BOOKS ON BUSINESS WRITING

Kenneth G. Brown, David J. Barton: "Brief Guide to Business Writing," Department of Management and Organizations, University of Iowa

Gary Blake, Robert W. Bly: "The Elements of Business Writing: A Guide to Writing Clear, Concise Letters, Memos, Reports, Proposals, and Other Business Documents," Longman, 1992

Maryann V. Piotrowski: "Effective Business Writing: A Guide For Those who Write On the Job," Collins, 2nd edition revised and updated, 1996

Barbara Minto: "The Minto Pyramid Principle: Logic in Writing, Thinking, & Problem Solving," Minto International, 1996

Graham Hart: "30 Minutes to Succeed in Business Writing," Kogan Page, 1997

Edward L. Smith, Stephen A. Bernhardt: "Writing At Work: Professional Writing Skills for People on the Job," McGraw-Hill, 1997

Edward P. Bailey Jr., Larry Bailey: "The Plain English Approach to Business Writing," Oxford University Press, 1997

Wilma Davidson: "Business Writing: What Works, What Won't," St. Martin's Griffin, 2001

Gerald J. Alred, Charles T. Brusaw, Walter E. Oliu: "The Business Writer's Handbook," St. Martin's Press, 2003

Shirley Taylor: "Model Business Letters, E-mails & Other Business Documents," FTPH, 2003

Jack E. Appleman: "10 Steps to Successful Business Writing (10 Steps)," ASTD Press, 2008

BOOKS ON SOCIAL PSYCHOLOGY AND BEHAVIORAL ECONOMICS

Robert B. Cialdini: "Influence: The Psychology of Persuasion," First Collins Business Essentials, edition 2007

Richard H. Thaler and Cass R. Sunstein: "Nudge: Improving Decisions about Health, Wealth, and Happiness," Penguin Books, 2009

About The Author

Herman Vantrappen has been a consultant with Arthur D. Little for more than 20 years. Currently he is a Director of the firm. Founded in 1886 in Cambridge, Massachusetts, Arthur D. Little is a global management consultancy, linking strategy, innovation and technology to ensure business success for its clients.

Herman Vantrappen has also been the editor-in-chief of *Prism*, the firm's bi-annual journal that is distributed to a large group of senior executives in industry and the public sector worldwide (see www.adl.com/insights/prism/). With eleven articles published in Prism, he has been one of its most prolific contributors, writing on topics such as business strategy, innovation management and government policy. He has also conducted and published interviews with the Chief Executive Officers of global corporations such as Heineken, Atlas Copco and Henkel. Furthermore, he has ghost-written and edited several other articles in Prism.

In addition, Herman Vantrappen has authored many pieces in a wide variety of other journals, magazines and newspapers. Several of these have been translated into Dutch, Spanish and Portuguese. He has appeared and spoken on television, radio and at conferences. He is also the author of numerous white papers and manuscripts addressed to the general public, private clients or an internal Arthur D. Little audience. For one of those, he was the recipient of the firm's much-coveted President's Award.

Herman Vantrappen obtained an M.B.A. from Carnegie-Mellon University's Tepper School of Business (Pittsburgh, USA) and an M.S. in Engineering from Leuven University (Leuven, Belgium).

www.ingramcontent.com/pod-product-compliance
Lightning Source LLC
Chambersburg PA
CBHW071234170526
45165CB00003B/1089